MISSION and MIGRATION

Papers read at the biennial conference of the
British and Irish Association for Mission Studies
at Westminster College, Cambridge
2nd – 5th July 2007

Editor
Stephen Spencer

cliff
COLLEGE
PUBLISHING

ISBN 978-1-898362-39-5
© 2008 Cliff College Publishing

British Library Cataloguing in Publication Data.
A catalogue record for this book is available
from the British Library.

**Cliff College Publishing,
Calver, Hope Valley, Derbys S32 3XG**

Printed by:

MOORLEY'S Print & Publishing
23 Park Rd., Ilkeston, Derbys DE7 5DA
✕⊃   Tel/Fax: (0115) 932 0643   ⊂✕
from data supplied on electronically

Contents

Contributors   5

Preface   6

Biblical perspectives

1. Mission, Migration and the stranger in our midst
   Tim Naish   7

Charting mission through migration

2. African Christians in Europe
   Gerrie ter Haar   31

3. Nigerian Pentecostal Missionary enterprise in Kenya:
   Taking the Cross over *Philomena Mwaura*   53

4. Mission perspectives among Pentecostal West Indian
   religious communities in New York City and London
   Janice McLean   79

5. The Hindu Diaspora in the UK: Insights and Challenges for
   Christian Mission *Israel Selvanayagam*   95

6. Non-western Christian missionaries in England:
   Has mission been reversed? *Rebecca Catto*   109

7. Mission and Home-Making: Church Expansion
   through Migration in the Democratic Republic of Congo
   Emma Wild-Wood   119

8. Hospitality and 'Hanging Out': Churches' engagement
   with people seeking asylum in the UK
   Susanna Snyder   129

Changing Christian Thinking

9. Exile, seeking asylum in the UK and the *Missio Dei*
   Nicholas Sagovsky   141

10. Rethinking 'migration' and 'mission'
    Timothy Gorringe   159

11. Multicultural Worship: Theological reflections
    on experience *Thomas R. Whelan*   173

BIAMS

Reflecting Christian witness globally

The British and Irish Association for Mission Studies is an inter-confessional body founded in 1990 as a forum for academic teachers, missionary practioners and others interested in Christian mission.

It publishes a twice-yearly bulletin and holds day conferences and biennial residential conferences.

Details of membership can be obtained from
> The Secretary,
> c/o The Henry Martyn Centre,
> Westminster College,
> Cambridge
> CB3 OAA

or from the website www.biams.org.uk

CONTRIBUTORS

Rebecca Catto is a research student with the University of Exeter.

Timothy Gorringe is Professor of Theology in the Department of Theology and Religious Studies, University of Exeter.

Gerrie ter Haar is Professor in the Institute of Social Studies, The Hague.

Janice McLean is a research student with the University of Edinburgh.

Philomena Mwaura is Senior Lecturer in the Dept of Philosophy and Religious Studies, Kenyatta University, Nairobi.

Tim Naish is Director of Studies on the Oxford Ministry Course, based at Ripon College, Cuddesdon.

Nicholas Sagovsky is Canon Theologian of Westminster Abbey and Visiting Professor of Theology and Public Life, Liverpool Hope University.

Israel Selvanayagam is Principal of the United Theological College, Bangalore.

Susanna Snyder is a priest in London and research student with the University of Birmingham.

Stephen Spencer is Director of Studies on the Northern Ordination Course and Yorkshire Ministry Course, based at the College of the Resurrection, Mirfield, and Publications Secretary of BIAMS.

Thomas R. Whelan is Associate Professor at Milltown Institute where he lectures in Liturgical and Sacramental Theology and is Dean of the Faculty of Theology and Spirituality. He is Chair of BIAMS.

Emma Wild-Wood is editor of the SPCK International Study Guides and recently secretary of BIAMS.

PREFACE

The chapters in this book represent papers delivered at the 2007 Cambridge conference of the British and Irish Association for Mission Studies. The full title of the conference was 'Strangers in Our Midst: Mission and Migration'. This title is alluded to by several of the papers. Each paper both describes aspects of migration in the world today, and reflects on them from a missiological point of view. However some papers concentrate on description and analysis of what is going on, and others concentrate on reflection. This book separates these two kinds of paper and presents each in turn. The descriptive and analytical papers are presented in the section 'Charting mission through migration'. The more reflective papers are presented in the section 'Changing Christian thinking'. The first chapter opens up some of the Biblical background to this hugely important and timely subject.

BIAMS would like to express its thanks to Cliff College Publishing for making it possible to produce this volume.

Biblical Perspectives

Chapter One

Mission, Migration and the stranger in our midst

Tim Naish

This chapter begins with a personal experience, for two reasons: one, that it is helpful to most readers to know something about where an author is coming from; and two, in all thinking and reflection about migration they will be determined that the actual experience of migrants, strangers, aliens – their joys and pains, their trials and discoveries, the heart's aches and the heart's ease – should not be forgotten.

A Personal Introduction

From 1980 to 2000 I served under the auspices of the Church Mission(ary)[1] Society in three continents. Among the people whose theology nourished my mission infancy were the leaders of what may be called a CMS tradition, like Max Warren, whose son-in-law Roger Hooker was my guide and guru at the Selly Oak Colleges, and John V. Taylor. I worked first in south India, then as a Mission Partner in Britain, in the Parish of Waterloo around its London Head Office. From 1993 for seven years I was in Uganda. But the personal story I begin with was the end of three and a half years from 1988 in Lubumbashi, in south eastern Zaïre (as the country was then called).

---

1 During this time it changed its name from *Church Missionary Society* to *Church Mission Society*.

During the central months of 1991, in the declining years of the Mobutu regime, the nation suffered a series of outbreaks of social chaos, shooting, rioting and looting - there was little loss of life - in its major cities, mostly led by soldiers who had not been paid for months. Lubumbashi, the second city, was the last to be hit. Just as we thought we would escape, one October night the place erupted in volleys of gunfire and destruction. Here's part of what I wrote the following day:

> The central moment and guiding image of what I have to describe is, has to be, one of movement: a turbulent river of animated people flowing down the main road west out of Lubumbashi centre, a road very familiar to me but become new this morning. A great mix of people, yes mostly young men but with plenty of women and some older people. A few people by themselves but mostly in twos or threes, talking very loudly, almost excessively brightly, as though covering something. At times it is hard to tell who is with whom, so densely are they coming.

> What is distinctive is that they are all burdened. Many carry on their backs big bundles of clothes or blankets baled up in hoops, forcing their faces downwards. But the loads are very varied: a half of a bicycle, a big radio, a sheet of corrugated roofing metal, a large electric fan, a small fridge, a precarious balance of three chairs, a bag of shoes, sports equipment, an inverted table... In my innocence, I think at first it is an exodus, people fleeing the shooting that has gone on during the night, salvaging what they can of their belongings. But after a minute I realise that they have gone into the city centre and are returning with whatever they have been able to grab from the mess there. Hence their boisterousness, the spring in the step. They are - at least for today - winners, bearing home their prizes.

Not quite a scene of migration, as we'd usually define it, but something with many relations to it. It led to our emigration from Zaire. It also led me to years of reflection on themes of exile, including the writing of a doctoral thesis on metaphors of displacement as a key field of imagery for the theology of mission.

Just let me invite you to ponder the context of this narrative, a reminder of the complexities of speaking of migration: my family and I were there as voluntary migrants from a quite different context – we had crossed continents to be there; the bishop with whom I was working was from a tribe whose natural territory had been carved apart by colonists between Rwanda, Uganda, and the Congo, so that he had been born in one, trained in the second, and was working in the third; the senior pastor within the Diocese was a Zambian who had moved years previously to work in the copper mines; others were from the neighbouring (ethnically and linguistically different) Zairean province and had similarly moved because of the mining industry; the rioting soldiers would have come from all over the country, especially the very distant areas which were Mobutu's stronghold. So we see a wide range of voluntary and involuntary migrants, and in both categories a variety of motivations. This complexity will have to be kept in mind in what follows. For we are well aware that this one particular now rather dated bundle of experiences is re-enacted in variegated forms across the world today. Immigration – which perforce also means there has been emigration - is news, and often rather hot news.

So after this introduction to both my own context and to the wider global setting in which we consider the conference theme, I intend in the first part of the paper to present some kind of biblical overview in four Old Testament movements and three New Testament trajectories, and in the second (after a very brief interlude) to suggest four more pervasive themes.

A Biblical Overview

I have debated whether to spell out formal biblical principles or theses in relation to migration. I have decided not to, for two main reasons: first that any principles one can adduce are likely *either* to be so vacuous and wide-ranging as to be unnecessary to put before intelligent people, *or* to be dangerous because in their efforts to be precise enough to avoid such vacuity they do not take the complexities of specific contexts sufficiently into account; and second that the production of theses would be likely to be based upon the predetermination by me of the aspects of mission and migration that I thought worthy of our attention. I for one hope, for example, that while we shall cover seriously some of the pressing issues of concern for immigration policy in Europe and elsewhere, and the cultural dimensions of migration, we shall not pursue that agenda exclusively.

My third reason is that in any case the *first* chapter of a book like this one has certain advantages of which I intend to take hold: one can perhaps be expected not to resolve issues or provide answers but to establish territory, to raise questions, to lay out some items for the agenda.

So I prefer to set out seven dimensions of scriptural material which pertain to our subject. Doubtless some of the interpretative directions in which I would wish to head will be discernable and provide something for you to react for or against. It is apparent that the topic is large, and I fully expect there to be aspects of it about which you find me frustratingly silent, and biblical references which you are astonished that I omit.

Expulsion

One might almost say that the narratives of Genesis 1-11 use the possibility of migration to describe the human condition. The gift of mobility - two legs, the dominion over beasts of burden, the skill to make arks - becomes the vehicle of loss. These are stories of impulsion and expulsion. Adam and Eve, man and woman, are enforced emigrants from the land of Eden, immigrants to the land of tillage and toil. Cain is driven out to the Land of Nod, that place of uncertainty for which Westermann in his Genesis commentary suggests the translation, the 'Land of the Restless Life'[2]. Noah his family and other animals become the archetypal boat people. All this culminates in the dispersal from Babel, the scattering of humankind in some kind of universal 'ur-migration', the paradigm of that confusion and failure of communication which accompanies the large-scale movement of human communities.

What are we to make of this? There is something very primal about our relationship to space we inhabit, in which we construct a sense of place, the land upon which we stand and move. We should not be surprised that questions of migration provoke and prove emotive. We are creatures, who share with others the territorial instinct and the

---

2 C. Westermann, *Genesis 1-11: a Commentary* (London: SPCK, 1984), 314.

defensiveness of our space. As with our other basic attributes –
sexuality, for example, or the capacity to speak – the richness with
which we are blessed is at the same time the root of our curse.

These short but vital chapters before the coming into being of a
chosen people serve as a vital foundation for faith's affirmation of a
shared humanity. There is a time and a space prior to the allocation or
possession of territory. If the defence of that which is 'ours' has any
legitimate grounds, they are not going to be those of inherent
superiority or a right which pertains to us at the level of our most basic
human existence which other women or men do not have. We are all
Babel people, equally implicated in the storming of heaven. This
assertion is necessary because attentive ears will from time to time
discern such claims lurking behind some expressions of opinion on
issues of migration and the use of land, even in our contemporary
world.

Evocation

The call of Abram - it is tempting to call it his 'evocation', in the
original sense of a calling out or calling forth, in order to provide a
schema of four O.T. movements each beginning with the letter E –
brings us a migration which in terms of its theological direction is
contrary and sets in motion what one might characterise as a train of
such movements for the sake of the other, for the sake of the divine
name, for the sake of blessing, which marks out God's mission and
God's people. If the expulsions of Genesis 1-11 draw out the pain of
leaving one's place, the journeys which Abraham and his descendants
make evoke its excitement. In all our discussion here this will be an
important dynamic to maintain. Without minimising the desperate
cruelties of so much of the human displacement in our world, we hold
on with gratitude to the possibilities which migration also opens out for
human flourishing and encounter. While it is generally fair to link the
former with the kind of enforced migration which accompanies
violence, drought, political injustice and the like, and the latter with
free and voluntary migration, there are sometimes surprises and often
elements of suffering and of something more positive in the same
experience.

In his attempt to identify 'the theme of the Pentateuch', David
Clines writes of a parallel though not identical paradox:

Something deeper [than a mere literary 'device'] about our view of man [*sic*] is implied by our cultural inheritance of travel stories and our continuing creation of them. Let me suggest that our love of travel stories springs from the desire of the unsettled to be settled, and of the settled to be unsettled. That is, the rootless identify with the travellers who search for a home, and the secure identify with the travellers who leave home. The human reality at the core of this twofold desire is not simple dissatisfaction with the way things are, whether on the part of the settled or of the unsettled, but an expression of the tension within the unsettled and the settled to be both - to encompass both experiences.[3]

The history and practice of Christian mission, its advances and its pitfalls, are full of reminders of this kind of ambiguous relation to place as part of the human condition.

Exodus

You will have guessed that my other two O.T. 'Es' are exodus and exile. Such has been the rediscovery of exodus as a missional theme over the last half century or so that to attempt a brief summary seems ridiculous. You will each be aware of some small parts of the literature. For our purposes, obvious as it is, might I point out how in the telling of this story of migration so many of the matters that we find commonly present in the cases of refugees, seekers of asylum, economic and other migrants are interwoven: matters of land – left and longed for, matters of identity (related in manifold ways to kinship, race, culture, religion…), matters of memory and of hope, matters of flight from oppression and fragile relationship with new neighbours. There is rarely any simple reading off, from the narratives of the biblical exodus, clear prescriptions for today's ills at the levels of policy; but there is the pivotal affirmation of the Lord's active will for good for the downtrodden and oppressed.

You will be aware of widespread debate among biblical scholars and historians in recent decades as to how much of the biblical exodus

---

3 Clines, *The Theme of the Pentateuch* (Journal for the Study of the Old Testament Supplement Series,10; Sheffield: JSOT Press, 1978), 107.

account has a basis in historical events. Some believe it has virtually none, that the narratives as we have them are a development over the centuries of powerful myths of the rise of one group of distinctive worshippers within the land. Others assert the substantial historicity of the events they describe; and between the two poles there are many mediating points of view. The very arguments make clear, whatever position one takes, the powerful nexus of migration and identity. 'When Israel was a child, I loved him, and out of Egypt I called my son' (Hosea 11:1). The exodus from Egypt and the giving of the law at Sinai create a people. Whether in the happening, in the memory or in the imagination, the telling and enacting of the story of the migrant people becomes the key and defining point of her existence. The binding of Israel to Yahweh in covenant is founded on his act of disruptive liberation. 'You have seen what I did to the Egyptians, and how I bore you on eagles' wings and brought you to myself. Now therefore, if you will obey my voice and keep my covenant, you shall be my own possession...' (Exodus 19:4-5). Notice that the flight from oppression, the wilderness time and the subsequent struggle for land, shape, purpose - including what is clearly a complex history of relationship to Canaanite religion and culture – come to be construed as a journey towards Yahweh. It is a story of great trial and cost, but also of great promise. It is also, like most stories, the tale of those who have come through; it is neither the Egyptian nor the Canaanite story of the 'exodus' and the 'conquest', and if it were it might have other names.

'There is no paradigm more central to Judaism than Exodus and Sinai... There is also no paradigm that should be more central to Christian self-understanding,' writes David Tracy[4] 'Yahweh who delivered you from Egypt' is as fundamental a memory of the Hebrew God as is 'the God and Father of our Lord Jesus Christ' of the God of the New Testament. His people are formed in their uprooting from the place of slavery.

I hope it goes almost without saying – but I shall say it – that we should not forget the this-worldly and political implications of the narrative and spiritualise it too quickly. Rooted in this story of the

---

4 D. Tracy, 'Exodus: Theological Reflection', in B. van Iersel & A. Weiler (eds.), *Exodus - A Lasting Paradigm* (Concilium 189, 118-124; Edinburgh: T & T Clark, 1987), 118.

freedom of oppressed people, the people of God must stand in memory alongside the displaced and marginalised. When

> ...tempted to depoliticise its self-understanding and praxis anew, Christians need only reflect on Exodus as the paradigm which should inform and transform the highly personal but not individualist Christian self-understanding in the reality of the death and resurrection of Jesus Christ.[5]

We are so used to an entirely spiritual appropriation of this story that it is hard to appreciate how abnormal is such a reading of the text. In saying this I do not wish to deny the profound metaphorical resonances of the narratives, but to assert a need for a resistance to a disengaged spirituality and mission.

Exile

The final great foundational and formational migration of the O.T. is in the exile to Babylon, or perhaps we should rather say the exile and return. Warned by the exile of the northern kingdom to Assyria one hundred and thirty years earlier, the people of Judah nonetheless continue to live in the land as possession rather than as gift – to use terms developed in the familiar analysis of Walter Brueggemann, whom I suspect is most missiologist's favourite O.T. theologian. They seek to control the land as a place of security and self-preservation, to 'eliminate the very precariousness which is at the centre of covenantal existence in or out of the land.'[6] In other words they cease to live in a spirit of displacement even when literal displacement is not their lot. No longer do they have a sense of their oddity among the nations as the people who bear the name of Yahweh, who are heading in a different direction.

So they are brought up short by a fresh and heart-breaking experience of migration, this time not to liberation but to seeming enslavement. Yet once more the moment of disruptive crisis proves to be creative. It has become widely accepted among scholars of the Hebrew Bible that the most intensive period in its formation was in or

---

5 *Ibid.*, 119.

6 W. Brueggemann, *The Land* (London: SPCK/Philadelphia, PA: Fortress Press, 1977), 76.

around the time of exile.[7] The radical rethink of what Yahweh was doing with them which their displacement necessitated led to new reflection and fresh perception of his way.

> The richness of the differing reactions to the events [of exile], and of the understanding of the nature of restoration, shows how deep an impression was made upon the community by the period, and how fertile were the minds which interpreted what happened and what they understood to be the outcome of the events.[8]

Perhaps it was only a few prophets - the Jeremiahs, the Ezekiels, the 'Isaiahs' of the exile - who began to perceive that God's hand might be in this after all. But slowly their voices were heard and appreciated; it is their words and the response to them that became Scripture. They[9] see that God displaces his people for the sake of his name (to use Ezekiel's language), that Israel has failed to such an extent in her missionary task of showing among the nations, by faithful covenantal living, the nature of Yahweh, that he has to act. They recognise in his punishment the seeds of their renewed liberation; as he has cut them off for the sake of his name so they will be restored for the same name's sake.

> The exile is seen as judgement upon the people's life, but more than that it is understood as lying within the purposes of God not simply as judgement but in relation to what he is doing in the life of the world.[10]

It is not surprising that in this new crisis the prophets should use the exodus as a model of Yahweh's activity (see for example Isaiah 51 and Ezekiel 20). Life in Babylon and its empire is a second wilderness, but one in which again Yahweh is present, transforming it from the ground of desolation to the place of hope. Isaiah's blossoming wilderness

---

7   So that, e.g., J.G. McConville can now write of '[g]enerations of scholars' who 'have thought of the exile as decisive in the formation of the literature...' in V.P. Long (ed.), *Israel's Past in Present Research: Essays on Ancient Israelite Historiography* (Winona Lake, IA: Eisenbrauns, 1999), 520.

8   P. Ackroyd, *Exile and Restoration* (London: SCM Press, 1968), 233.

9   There is clearly a danger in seeming thus to isolate a single point of view; nonetheless what follows is surely one major strand that emerges from reflection on the exile.

10 Ackroyd, *op. cit.*, 234.

mirrors Jeremiah's and Ezekiel's transformed hearts. Again it takes the experience of radical dislocation to refresh God's people's vision of him and of his pattern for the world of which they are the witnesses.

What is more surprising is that the language and theology of exile have been so little taken up in the Christian tradition:

> It is, without doubt, the great biblical theme with which Christians have been least able to identify themselves, even during the periods of their fiercest persecution. How many Christian hymns, for instance, have made use of the imagery of Exile? This testifies to the buoyancy we derive from our faith in the resurrection of Jesus, but also, less happily, to a facile triumphalism which has disqualified us from entering into either the spiritual insights of Judaism or the Passion of God.[11]

Even in the fifteen years since that was published, I think one can discern signs of the recovery of exilic imagery which Taylor invites. Does this result from the increasing marginalisation of the churches in western societies,[12] even if of course it has to be admitted that this is a process which had been going on for many decades before he wrote?

We tend to think of the experience and rhetoric of exile as coming to an end with the Old Testament, if not before. But in his work on the context and message of Jesus, N.T. Wright has drawn attention to the continuing sense of alienation, displacement and expectation that persisted in his day. For example:

> Most Jews of this period, it seems, would have answered the question "where are we?" in language which, reduced to its simplest form, means: we are still in exile. They believed that, in all the senses which mattered, Israel's exile was still in progress. Although she had come back from Babylon, the glorious message of the prophets remained unfulfilled. Israel

---

11 J.V. Taylor, *The Christlike God* (London: SCM Press, 1992), 18f.

12 There is evidence that this is happening even in the fifteen or so years since Taylor wrote. E.g: 'I agree with recent suggestions, especially by John Howard Yoder, Walter Brueggemann, and Stanley Hauerwas, that an "exilic theology" promises to be the most provocative, creative and helpful set of ideas that modern Christians can derive from the ancient Hebrews' religious reflections on their experiences.' D. Smith-Christopher, *A Biblical Theology of Exile* (Minneapolis, MN: Fortress Press, 2002), 6.

remained in thrall to foreigners; worse, Israel's God had not returned to Zion.[13]

Consequently, Wright interprets the 'prodigal son' as a story primarily about exile and restoration: to those who recognise what is happening in and around Jesus' own ministry, the prodigal love of God is now fulfilling the promise of return from the far country, while those who grumble at it and him are effectively like Samaritans, those who never went into exile and oppose the return.[14] Wright's project is ongoing, and questions have been raised about his reading of the inter-testamental evidence. But he alerts us to the resonance of imagery of exile, displacement, sojourning, in New Testament times as well as Old.

Moreover, sensitive reflection on exile recognises that the Jews began there a wrestling with the experiences of migration and a struggle to see God in them which has continued to the present. In his moving account of the history of the interpretation of the exile and diaspora of his people, called *Galut* (Hebrew for exile), Yitzhak Baer reminds us of the way the early Christians appropriated the idea and ignored, and then persecuted, the Jews:

> In the teaching of the Fathers, the historic role of God's people is taken over in the concept of the Civitas Dei, which consists of the secretly chosen ones who wander in pilgrimage through the world. The meaning of the word 'Galut,' in its dual aspect of religious propaganda and of suffering for the sake of humanity's redemption, is given to the idea of the Civitas Dei, while the true Galut of the Jewish people, stripped of its meaning as sacred history, of the drama of salvation, becomes an object of contempt and ridicule.[15]

Baer made out a case for a Zionist understanding of 'Galut', but for many Israel's exile has never ended, and the church needs to give renewed and repentant attention to that experience, ready to learn from it. Let this small example be one reminder that our theme is not one to

---

13 N.T. Wright, *The New Testament and the People of God* (London: SPCK, 1992), 268-9.

14 N.T. Wright, *Jesus and the Victory of God* (London: SPCK, 1996), 125-131.

15 Y. Baer, *Galut* (New York: Schocken Books, 1947), 14. [Original edition in German, 1936, Berlin: Schocken].

be discussed by the Christian church in isolation, but in dialogue and shared action with others, across religious traditions.

The 'Stranger in our midst'?

Tom Wright has helped us to cross the bridge between the testaments. The N.T. offers us less obvious material for our theme, but no less important. I offer three reflections, very roughly corresponding to sections or genres of the N.T.

We can begin from Barth's well known handling of the incarnation under the heading, 'The Way of the Son of God into the Far Country'[16]:

> But [God] does not hold aloof. In being gracious to man [*sic*] in Jesus Christ, He also goes into the far country, into the evil society of this being which is not God and against God. He does not shrink from him. He does not pass him by as did the priest and the Levite the man who had fallen among thieves. He does not leave him to his own devices. He makes his situation his own.[17]

Metaphors of movement to describe the relations of Jesus Christ to God and to the world have strong New Testament roots (principally the language of coming and going, sending and being sent, in John) and not surprisingly therefore flourish in later accounts of incarnation: 'He came down from heaven'. From the beginnings of Christianity, reflection on the Christ centred around and between the two poles of the divine-human axis, and it was perhaps natural that metaphors of place and movement were widely used. Is it too fanciful to speak of God's migrant worker? The main suggestion I would like to make is that this one who comes among us both is, and is not, a stranger. He came to his own, but his own did not accept him. The gospels bear witness to one who was familiar, who grew up in an ordinary home in Nazareth, whose brothers and sisters were known, and yet who defied category and rank, who constantly surprised, who was like a visitor

---

16 K. Barth, *Church Dogmatics* (Edinburgh: T & T Clark, 1936-69) IV, 1, 157-210 - though in the exposition itself Barth makes little of the image derived from Luke 15. Cf. also 'The Homecoming of the Son of Man' in IV, 2, 20-154.

17 *Ibid.*, IV, 1, 158-9.

from elsewhere in his flouting of the society's standard and patterns, who was from the culture and yet beyond it.

Looked at in this light is Jesus of Nazareth the paradigm of stranger in our midst who forces us to wrestle with the quandaries of human situatedness, who confronts our Babels and reveals them for what they are? Is he the one who hovers between the alien and the familiar and thus challenges both our perception of ourselves and our relations with the other, with the one who is different?

Here are a few pieces of evidence from the gospels. The story of the virgin birth, whatever its origin, is a narrative which accounts for a child who is both ordinary and strange. He is born in Nazareth, amidst migration because of the mechanisms of imperial control, and as for many in such circumstances there is only temporary and barely adequate shelter. As a child he becomes a migrant, a refugee, fleeing from tyranny and violence, as his family run to Egypt for his safety's sake. It is consonant with the reality of life as a displaced person that we know nothing of that time. Such people are always hidden in their individuality, are today at best a statistic or an aid agency symbol. He shares this common fate and yet differently, for were it not for his coming this particular threat to the infant boys would not exist. We have stories of startling otherness as a twelve year old, of the encounter with wilderness, of his chosen homelessness, with nowhere to lay his head, of his constant movement away from power and success. Strikingly he says that the prophet is not accepted among the prophet's own people. We have some evidence of his own struggling with the questions of identity, race, belonging, and the love of God – 'It is not fair to take the children's food and throw it to the dogs.'

Like the narratives of his birth, those of his transfiguration point to an otherness, record that sense that those who met him and followed discovered a man whom they knew but who was also strange to them. Finally the stranger in the midst is so uncomfortable that he must die for the sake of the people, and he is put to death outside the city in rejection and revilement. For his crucifixion on the hill 'outside the camp', as Hebrews puts it (13:11) is the culmination of his life. He dies in the unclean place, where the carcasses of the bull and the goat slaughtered to make atonement are burnt - in what would be, outside the camp of Leviticus, literally the wilderness. He offers a model of the displaced life, which is also a missional life.

So I suggest that the life and death of Jesus of Nazareth, his resurrection life, offer us a model for life with and for the strangers in our midst, both by virtue of his embodying that strangeness in confounding and truth-revealing ways, and also by virtue of his dealing with and for the strangers to whom he gave himself. His disciples find the Christ lives out in himself and makes possible for others a resolution of that quest for an identity which is so secure in the love of the God he calls Father that it subverts the alienations which abound, around and within us.

The Followers of Christ as Aliens and Strangers

Although Jesus himself is not in the gospels described in terms of being foreign or alien or an outsider – words such as *paroikos* or *xenos* are not used of him - I have tried to claim that his behaviour and his teaching sometimes make him seem like one. And so perhaps it's not surprising that this is one way that his followers develop for speaking of themselves. It is not frequent or pervasive, but it does seem to cross trajectories within the earliest Church. We find it in Hebrews, in 1 Peter, and outside the N.T. most famously in the Epistle to Diognetus. It is echoed in Pauline thought if not in the precise vocabulary. Those in Christ are citizens of heaven but ambassadors to the earth where we live (Pauline), at home in the body and therefore in exile from the Lord (Paul again), longing for one country, with a city prepared, while sojourning in another (the language of Hebrews), aliens and strangers in the world (Petrine).

What are we to make of this? For one thing, it seems to justify a continuation by parallel from the O.T. into the New of that tradition in which, by virtue of themselves having been resident aliens in Egypt and recipients of their land of promise as gift rather than as possession, the people of God are charged and obliged by law to show especial grace and care to the foreigners resident among them (Leviticus 19). Those who know themselves to be foreigners incorporated by grace (and in this sense – Eph. 2:19 – Paul or his follower *does* use the language) are to agents of loving inclusiveness. All of this might of course be inferred from the commandment to love, but there are here grounds for reinforcing it and practising it with particular care in such contexts.

We can take this further by reference to one specific piece of exegesis. In the 1980s the American scholar J H Elliott wrote a book length study of 1 Peter called *A Home for the Homeless*, which I'm sure some of you will know – one of the pioneering works of sociological exegesis. Its major thesis was quite contentious and has certainly not won universal or even widespread acceptance, but even if not fully embraced raises an important issue. The letter addresses its recipients as *paroikoi* - exiles (NRSV) or strangers (NIV); often what Elliott calls a 'pilgrim theology' is built upon notions derived from such language of Christians as temporary residents of this passing world en route to their true home. You've probably preached such sermons, and he is not criticising them per se. But his analysis of *paroikos* and its related terms results in a claim that this is language with precise legally and socially defined meaning in the culture of the Hellenised Roman world to denote those with a 'resident alien' status. These are *paroikoi* not by virtue of their heavenly home but with regard to their condition in society.

This is not the place to evaluate the thesis in detail. Rather, it reminds us even in the possibility of its correctness of the danger of spiritualising the terms of migration and estrangement without getting to grips with their most urgent and obvious physical manifestations. Where we are to use such patterns of language as image and metaphor it must not be to the neglect of, but parallel with, their real and life-engaging meanings for millions of our fellow creatures.

> In 1 Peter the addressees were not being told that they had been made strangers by God's election but that they could find strength *to remain* strangers in the conviction of their divine election. By interpreting their condition in society as a divine vocation, however, 1 Peter suggests that social marginality and estrangement can be regarded by the Christians as not merely something tolerable but even desirable.[18]

That itself is a rather dangerous conclusion if one took it as applicable to all marginal groups in society today. But we should be

---

18   J.H. Elliott, *A Home for the Homeless* (London, SCM Press, 1982), 132.

thankful for this kind of reminder that to characterise our Christian vocation as 'aliens and strangers' is by no means to avoid the realities of societal, cultural, religious and embodied alienation.

Migration as Mission

Finally in this section, we must recall, on the basis primarily of the missionary journeys of Paul, that without migration there would have been very little mission, at least in human terms. The Matthean missionary command is explicitly migratory, and so is the Johannine unless one interprets the 'sending' of the disciples at the most metaphorical end of the spectrum of the possible range. It is worth reflecting also on the fact that Paul's journeys for the sake of the gospel were both (in the early cases) *voluntarily* undertaken, and yet also, if we take Acts as reasonably accurate, in the final instance *enforced* as he was transported to face trial in Rome. Thus was the gospel spread there and in places like Malta.

It is perhaps likely given our political and social context that, rightly, we shall focus in this book on the difficulties and the pains that the displacement of millions enacts in our world. However it would be sad indeed if as missiologists we had little time for the more positive dimensions of migration. Mostly we rejoice in, as we study, the lives and work of those who have travelled and settled in new places for the sake of the mission of God's kingdom. Most often these have been chosen and accepted vocations to migration. But attention has been drawn especially in recent decades to the extent to which involuntary displacement has been and is also a significant factor in the spread of the gospel and the work of Christian mission.

One area for discussion might well be the extent to which patterns of missional migration are changing. In many cases mission agencies, in this part of the world at least, are being forced to ask such questions in response to change in patterns of religious adherence, to political realities, to financial climates, to social conditions. It is often noted that the extent to which Paul envisaged his paths of missional movement as continuing and developing in the church is quite unclear. We know from our engagement with the history of mission just how multi-faceted the story of migration and Christian mission has been and will doubtless continue to be.

Interlude: Little Books with Big Things to Say

That ends a short glimpse at the big picture; before I go on to draw out a few themes from within that picture, it would be wrong of me given my brief not to remind you that, often at something of a tangent to the big picture (mixing my metaphors) there are what one might call little books with big things to say about mission and migration. I'm thinking particularly of Ruth, and of Esther and Lamentations and Jonah, and also, though easier to subsume within the bigger picture, of Ezra-Nehemiah. I can do no more than advert to their relevance, having reluctantly decided against a greater focus upon them at the expense of other things... I hope very much that others will come back to them.

Four Biblical Themes

I have steered one course through the major structures of the biblical story, in order to give some perspective on mission and migration within them; of course there could have been other ways of conducting the voyage. And if now I highlight even more briefly four themes, it is even more apparent that there could have been other choices, and I trust people will draw attention to my deficiencies.

The first theme is **the wilderness**, an evocation of place which has many connotations and faces. Often it is the place through which people have to pass; it is the place of transition, the space between Egypt and the promise land, and the space between Babylon and Jerusalem. It is the space through which Jesus has to go for his baptism in the Jordan to issue in fruitful ministry. It would be false to claim it too exclusively as the place of migration – there is more to it than that – but this is one important dimension of its meaning. Many of us, most of us I expect, have migrated seriously across cultures for a time. And of those who have I believe the great majority would admit to elements of that experience that were wilderness-like. What do I mean by that: that the migration included times of loneliness, of disorientation, questionings of purpose and identity; perhaps also vague shadows of threat. Most of us have probably been cushioned from the worst of this by wealth, welcome, friendship, power to make choices (including to leave, to return whence we came, if we wished). Also I mean that there has at the same time been a sense of test, the sense of place where God could be found. For the wilderness, the

23

place of barrenness, trial, wandering, the place that is no place, is the place where in the O.T. Yahweh reveals himself and binds himself to his people, thereby creating them in their distinctive role. "I am Yahweh your God from the land of Egypt; you know no God but me, and besides me there is no saviour. It was I who knew you in the wilderness, in the land of drought" (Hosea 13:4-5). We have opened ourselves to the possibility of this 'wilderness' (even if that was not primary in our perception of it) precisely because of that sense, as perhaps Jesus did. Many of these ambiguities in biblical evocation of wilderness might inform our thinking.

From a Christian – and also perhaps a Jewish – perspective, the Scriptures suggest that challenges to displacement form God's people, and in answering those challenges the sense of identity and mission develops. For in the subsequent tradition the wilderness becomes a sign of the people's response. It is either where they proved their faith - "Thus says Yahweh, I remember the devotion of your youth, your love as a bride, how you followed me in the wilderness, in a land not sown" (Jeremiah 2:2) - or it is the place of grumbling and despair where their inconstancy is revealed - "But the house of Israel rebelled against me in the wilderness; they did not walk in my statutes..." (Ezekiel 20:13). Whichever of these traditions is being used, it is true that the wilderness is the place where relationship to God, attitude to the world, and community character are being tested. Thus the place that is no place, the habitat of displacement, is also the place of God. It is the field of Yahweh's faithfulness, whether in drawing Israel to him or in restraining his hand against her waywardness. So the desert has continued to exercise an important role, both practical and symbolic, in Christian spirituality. It has become the sign of what we might call the migratory spirit, a pre-eminent place for Christians to live out as a signal to others the necessity of a way that is out of place in this world.

If such a spirit is one that we recognise for ourselves, what does it mean for us in handling issues of migration for others? We must proceed with care: so I trust it will be understood that I'm not advocating say counselling the inmate of an immigration detention centre who is threatened with deportation to her place of origin, 'Cheer up, a bit of a wilderness experience will do you good.' No, we recognise the sheer terror of many wilderness places, and in our accompanying of others within them will have to confront rather than collude with the sources of terror.

We need to be in touch with the wilderness as a reflection of Jesus' own frequent return to the lonely place, the place of prayer, often the place of struggle and resolve, often the place of encounter and refreshment and new strength. And we need to be opening up such places for others, for individuals and communities. These places, both for ourselves and for others, will be both literal and metaphorical.

My second suggestion for a theme I can best sum up as **Jeremiah 29 versus Psalm 137**. You will quickly I think identify those references as containing two conflicting attitudes to the people of God's enforced migration in Babylon. The psalm describes especially poignantly the pain of those whose memories of home draw forth bitter tears as they are asked to sing – to adapt, to inculturate, to integrate, do we infer? – in the place of their exile. It ends with a curse the strength of which has regularly embarrassed commentators in its frank invocation of violence against the children of the oppressors. Yet it accurately reflects the kind of human feelings that situations of aggressive displacement regularly produce and the kind of human actions which we see all too often in places of ethnic cleansing.

Jeremiah on the other hand, in opposition to false prophets whom we infer were urging some kind of resistance movement, urges co-operation: 'Seek the welfare of the city where I have sent you into exile, and pray to Yahweh on its behalf, for in its welfare you will find your welfare' - scarcely compatible with the dashing of its children against the rocks. Transferred to contemporary debate, we seem as it were to have conflicting biblical advice about which cricket team an immigrant to this country from India or Pakistan might support. Jeremiah may appear not an inappropriate advocate of the barmy army, even if he was no Norman Tebbit.

The debate about Israel's attitudes to the nations is of course very far-reaching and leads us biblically into matters such as deuteronomistic annihilation of peoples, the purpose of the book of Jonah, Ezra's fierceness about marriage outside the community, the context and purpose of the book of Ruth, the debate between Nehemiah and Sanballat and Co. about being loyal to one's own community's memory and identity and loyal to a distant government.

There is no space to chew at any of this, only to signal how much is on the table in front of us. The N.T. version of this paradox is that embodiment in practice of an existence which is in the world but not of the world which has been so often the concern of missionaries and missiologists from John and Paul onwards.

A third theme develops my reflection upon Jesus as THE stranger in the midst, but picks up also on the rendering of Yahweh in the O.T. We might call it the theme of **the migrant God**. Can we speak of the Christian (and perhaps also the Jewish, though that's not for us to say) as the Migrant God? Donald MacKinnon in an essay contrasts Moses' God who is '...altogether strange, alien, inscrutable', who '...might destroy, or hide himself so totally that even a servant as devoted to his God's cause as Moses might feel himself forsaken', with Aaron's golden calf which will 'neither forsake nor destroy, as Moses' God might'[19]. This gives a flavour of the distinctiveness of Yahweh. True, modern scholarship no longer allows us to take easily at face value such a radical distinction of character between Yahweh and other deities of that place and time as the O.T. suggests[20]; nevertheless the picture which the O.T. as a whole presents does stand out as one of a God whose freedom from local attachment and control, whose sovereignty and universal concern, whose refusal to be tied down by image or shrine, marks him out. The tradition of Yahweh's presence going before them as cloud and fire (Exodus 13:21f etc.) becomes one of the great symbols of this mobility and of his sovereign protection of his people wherever they go. It used to be common to find the roots of this understanding of the divine nature in Israel's nomadic past. Although the historicity of this past is increasingly being questioned in O.T. study, there is still some point to Victor Maag's perception of the matter:

> This inspiring, guiding, protecting God of the nomads differs quite fundamentally in various respects from the gods of the agrarian peoples. The god of the nations is locally bound... The transmigration God of the nomads, however, is not bound

---

19 D. MacKinnon, *Themes in Theology: the Three-fold Cord* (Edinburgh: T & T Clark, 1987), 11.

20 See especially M. Smith, *The Early History of God* (San Francisco, CA: Harper & Row, 1990).

territorially and locally. He journeys along with them, is himself on the move.[21]

The more elusive side to Yahweh's nature is perhaps rather obscured by the deuteronomistic stress on the centralisation of the cult at Jerusalem which came to dominate, though the paradoxical nature of temple presence is recognised: "Behold, heaven and highest heaven cannot contain thee; how much less this house which I have built" (I Kings 8:27). At its best this tradition always held a sense of Yahweh's gracious condescension in allowing his name to dwell there; but prophetic traditions often provide a necessary corrective. Micah, Jeremiah and others are emphatic that the people cannot go on trusting in Yahweh's presence in his place (the temple) irrespective of their attitude to the covenantal commands; Ezekiel both encounters Yahweh's chariot in exile and sees the glory of Yahweh departing from the temple in stages in response to the sinfulness of the city. It is easy to overlook the fact that simply where the vision of chapter 1 happens is of radical significance: 'In short, a cascade of images declares Yahweh's mobility and his ability to be present in Babylon.'[22] This is underscored in the vivid account of the glory departing from Jerusalem (chs. 8-11), and then again by the vision of his return which sums up Ezekiel's hope for the future (43:1-5). The promises of return of the later part of the book of Isaiah continue the theme of Yahweh's mobility, casting the end of exile as a second exodus, the wilderness again as God's highway, the people again led forth in joy and peace. 'When you pass through the waters I will be with you' (43:2).

Exile forced on the people of God a radical reappraisal of the nature of their God and of his ways with them. They could go back to aspects of their traditions that were not just about God known in settlement and landedness, but about the pilgrim God going with them, displacing himself for their sake and for the sake of his name, because he had entrusted the one to the other. Dislocation became the ground of renewed mission.

---

21 V. Maag, 'Malkût Jhwh', in *Supplements to Vetus Testamentum VII* (Congress Volume, Oxford 1959), 139-40, translated and cited in J. Moltmann, *Theology of Hope*. (London: SCM Press, 1967), 96f.

22 R. Klein, *Israel in Exile: A Theological Interpretation* (Philadelphia, PA: Fortress Press, 1979), 74.

Exile was and is a catalyst for translating the faith. A Second Isaiah could take the traditions of the old exodus and the old Zion processions and say that God's word guaranteed a new Exodus and a new trip to Zion. God's presence had always been affirmed in Israel, but in the hands of an Ezekiel it became really good news for folks in exile.[23]

Returning for a moment to Jesus' ministry, recent scholarship has drawn attention to the socio-political factors at play. He comes from Galilee, a region peripheral to a province peripheral to the empire of the day. His life can be seen as an attack from the margins against centralised and static ways of seeing and being. In Sean Freyne's investigation of the significance of Jesus' Galilean provenance he concludes:

> The complex set of social and religious tensions within which Galilean life was lived in the first century was indeed fertile soil for the emergence of an alternative view of Jewish faith and practice; on the one hand this was deeply attached to and respectful of the central symbols of that faith, and yet, on the other hand it was constantly being drawn to break out of a narrow definition of the meaning of those symbols and to recognise their universal importance in religious terms... God's presence had been completely de-centred for the followers of Jesus and the system of observances that a localised understanding of that presence had sanctioned was thoroughly destabilised.[24]

A major characteristic of Jesus' ministry, his teaching and action, not separable from his way of being, is a challenge to the settled order, to things (and people) in their places as society - or the powerful in

---

23 *Ibid.*, 153.

24 S. Freyne, *Galilee, Jesus and the Gospels* (Minneapolis, MN: Fortress Press, 1988), 270. I give this quotation at some length because it implies processes that have often been observed in situations of Christian mission. The tension (often creative) between the global and the local is a frequent dynamic in mission, and the sense which Freyne conveys of the displacing effect of Jesus (note, an effect to which their setting, their placement, made them open) is often an aspect of missional existence. With regard to Galilee and marginality, in a specifically missional context, see also P. Hertig 'The Galilee Theme in Matthew: Transforming Mission through Marginality', in *Missiology* XXVI:1 (1998), 23-35.

society - wished them to be. The personal and the cultural or political dimensions of this challenge belong together.

The summation of this theme encourages us to remember the commonplace observation that in the face of the stranger, the migrant, we might see something of God himself. The characteristics of the person in need within Jesus' great eschatological picture of the scene before the throne of glory, in Matthew 25, are typically those of the displaced person: hunger, thirst, being a stranger, nakedness, sickness, imprisonment.

My fourth and last theme is simply an iteration of the biblical demand for **justice** for the alienated and marginalised. I accept there are those who would reject the whole thrust of liberation theology with its deeply missional dynamic. But rather as evangelical songs have widely influenced the church in this country even in places where their ethos is not swallowed wholesale, so the theology of liberation and its affirmation of divine bias to the poor (forgive me for speaking in catchphrases) has made its impact even in surprising places. In this I rejoice (I speak of liberational approaches, not of music in church!), though there is much more to be done in raising awareness and speaking out as Christian people on behalf of victims.

It is surely hard to read the Bible without gaining a sense that, in an age where millions are being displaced by war, oppression, drought and famine, or the inequities and iniquities systems of trade and economic organisation, followers of Christ should be deeply concerned. In situations where most basic needs – food, clothing, shelter, language, identity, belonging – are often not being met, practical love and care are demanded. But more than this, the factors that bring about these displacements have to be addressed.

In a messy world there are multiple competing justices and competing assertions of rights and needs for protection. We have to affirm I believe God's special concern for the aliens, the orphans and the widows (Deut. 14:29 etc.) and those like them in their vulnerability, and where justice for them seems to compete with justice for the established, the comfortable and those in possession, to know which side we are called to be on; while looking, as Jesus constantly did, to confound the confrontational logic which only thinks in terms of sides.

Conclusion[25]

I end with a quotation which picks up implicitly on that claim that the language of 'sides' is not always helpful, and thus reminds us of the complexities with which we shall be dealing in our reflection; for it draws attention to the way in which we are all 'Strangers to Ourselves', to use the title of the book which it begins. In considering mission and migration many of us may be tempted to think we are thinking only of those 'out there'; but Julia Kristeva, the influential Bulgarian-French theorist, psychoanalyst and semiotician writes:

> Foreigner: a choked up rage deep down in my throat, a black angel clouding transparency, opaque, unfathomable spur. The image of hatred and of the other, a foreigner is neither the romantic victim of our clannish indolence nor the intruder responsible for all the ills of the polis. Neither the apocalypse on the move nor the adversary to be eliminated for the sake of appeasing the group. Strangely, the foreigner lives within us: he is the hidden face of our identity, the space that wrecks our abode, the time in which understanding and affinity founder. By recognising him within ourselves, we are spared detesting him in himself. A symptom that precisely turns "we" into a problem, perhaps makes it impossible, the foreigner comes in when the consciousness of my difference arises, and he disappears when we all acknowledge ourselves as foreigners, unamenable to bonds and communities.'[26]

---

25 As delivered, the paper at this point offered a more extended concluding image: the complex weaving together of four warp strands of action (the pursuit of justice, the duty of care, the call to celebrate and name Christ, the recognition of our own non-objectivity) with four woof strands of belonging (matters of land, of race and community, of cultural and religious identity, and of memory and hope).

26 J. Kristeva *Strangers to Ourselves* (New York: Columbia University Press.1991), 1.

Charting mission through migration

Chapter 2

African Christians in Europe

Gerrie ter Haar

In the last few decades, Christianity in Europe has been given a new impulse as a result of migration by non-Western Christians. Many of these immigrants have founded new churches wherever they have settled, notably Christians from sub-Saharan Africa. This recent development therefore reflects a new phase in European church history, which deserves more scholarly attention than it currently receives.

In the early 1990s, I started to investigate the life of African-initiated churches in continental Europe, especially in the Netherlands, considering its implications for both the established churches and the host society at large.[1] At that time - and unlike Britain which has a much longer history of African-initiated churches - this was a novel topic, simply because the phenomenon itself was new and had come as a surprise to the secularised societies in which these churches emerged, as well as to the existing (white) Christian communities in the countries concerned. The latter, in my experience, often found it difficult to recognise the African Christians in their midst as 'proper'

---

1 See notably Gerrie ter Haar, *Halfway to Paradise: African Christians in Europe*, Cardiff Academic Press, 1998, a full-length pioneering study. The bibliography contains further references relevant to the subject matter, up to 1997.

Christians, people like them, since Africans' style of worship in many cases does not resemble conventional forms of Christian worship in traditional European congregations. This is especially so in regard to the spirit-oriented character of African-Christian worship. Sustained by a theology that lays emphasis on the power of the Holy Spirit, seemingly at the expense of the other dimensions of the Trinity, this continues to have an alienating effect on traditional congregations in Europe that both culturally and ideologically favour a rather different style. In the Netherlands, for example, whose particular conditions I know best, there is historically no significant Pentecostal trend. The traditional mainline churches are characterised by an intellectual approach that reveals a belief in the influence of the mind over the inclinations of the heart. We may perceive a historical background in which the Enlightenment has left its unmistakeable traces: Western cultures generally do not appreciate the loss of self-control that accompanies spirit-oriented behaviour. In our societies, a responsible, adult person should, ideally, stay in control of him- or herself under all circumstances; if not, such a person is declared ill, in need of psychological help, or otherwise incapable of taking care of themselves. Social esteem is accorded to persons who prove to be in full control of their own life. In Africa, on the other hand - and the same goes for many other societies in the world - social esteem may be attached to the ability to allow an external force to take over control for a certain period of time, especially to communicate with the spirit world, or otherwise to commune with the divine. In the case of African Christians, this means to communicate with God.

The way in which African Christians in Europe tend to communicate with God thus appears to hamper communication with their fellow-Christians in Europe. The latter seem to consider Africans' style of worship as a unique manifestation of their African culture - whatever this may be thought to be - as a result of which African Christians are encouraged to celebrate in their 'own' way, which is then of no or little consequence to European Christians. In the Netherlands, this has had the effect of further marginalising African Christians under the pretext of allowing cultural diversity in the church universal. In my book *Halfway to Paradise* I have argued that, in effect, Dutch Christians tend to see African Christianity mainly as another African indigenous religion.[2] This may be one reason why the relationship between European Christians and African Christians in Europe often continues to be considered in missionary or diaconal terms, rather than as an ecumenical relation.[3] The scholarly preoccupation of many Western academics with cultural identity is similarly prominent in research concerning African Christians in Europe. In this case, too, the emphasis is on the cultural expression of African Christianity rather than on the Christian content of African ideas. The paradoxical situation that results from this is that African Christians in Europe tend to emphasise what historically and ideologically *binds* them with their fellow Europeans, and Europeans tend to emphasise what *separates* African Christians from them. It is no surprise that this has certain consequences for the debate on mission and migration.

African migration

International migration forms the background against which to consider the current debate on mission and migration. The newly founded 'African churches' - as they are commonly known - are, one way or another, the product of the recent migration trends that are part of modern globalisation. Whereas in the past, many sub-Saharan Africans migrated to the metropoles of the former colonising powers, notably Britain and France, over the last two decades they have also migrated in substantial numbers to other parts of continental Europe, as a result of the political and economic crises in Africa.[4] While many Africans have arrived in Europe as political refugees, many more have

---

2 Ibid., notably pp. 82-6.

3 Cf. the Dutch report 'Geboren in Sion/Born in Sion' (June 2001), which provides a policy framework for the relation between the mainline churches in the Netherlands and the migrant churches. (Published bi-lingually by the national headquarters of the Uniting Churches in Utrecht, since 1 May 2004 known as the PKN, the Protestant Church in The Netherlands).

4 The International Organisation for Migration estimated in 2005 that of the 466 million documented Africans in the EU, an increasing number came from sub-Saharan Africa. The majority of these went to France and Britain, followed by Germany and Italy. Another 7-8 million undocumented African migrants were further estimated to live in the EU, mostly in southern Europe. See http://www.iom.int/.

come as labour migrants, mostly from West Africa.[5] Inasmuch as they are Christians, these African migrants have founded Christian congregations in the various places where they have settled. Since most of them came to Europe to find a job - or, to be more exact, to earn some money - they can be found in all the prosperous countries of Europe, including Germany and The Netherlands, or in regions of Europe that are less affluent but regularly need cheap labour for seasonal work, such as southern Italy and southern Spain. But even more recently, they are also found in Eastern Europe, sometimes as the result of a conscious mission strategy.[6] It appears that in spite of restrictive European migration policies, the presence of Africans has become a fact of life, and so has their religious life, of which the African-initiated churches are the most notable expression. Although this remains an under-researched issue, we know that many such churches exist in Germany, France, the Benelux and the Scandinavian countries, Spain, Italy, Portugal, Switzerland and - more recently - also in Ireland[7] (that in a short time has changed from an emigration into an immigration country), as well as in some of the countries of the former Soviet Union.

In conformity with recent African migration patterns, most of the African congregations in Europe have been founded by Ghanaians and Nigerians. According to migration statistics, Ghanaians are at the top of the list of West African countries from where people migrate to Europe.[8] At the time of my own research, in the mid-1990s, Ghana, Senegal and Nigeria were, in that order, the three most important countries producing emigrants from sub-Saharan Africa to Europe, providing 55% of the total West African immigrant population in the European Union (which at that time consisted of 15 member states

---

5   For recent figures, see Dirk Kohnert, 'African migration to Europe: obscured responsibilities and common misconceptions', 2007, accessible on www.giga-hamburg.de/content/publikationen/pdf/ wp49_kohnert.pdf.

6   A notable example is the Redeemed Christian Church of God, which has its headquarters in Nigeria. For a full-length study of this church, see Asonzeh F.-K. Ukah, *A New Paradigm of Pentecostal Power: A Study of the Redeemed Christian Church of God in Nigeria*, Trenton, NJ: Africa World Press (in press).

7   As recorded in a recent study by Abel Ugba, *Shades of Belonging: African Pentecostals in 21st-century Ireland*, forthcoming with Africa World Press, Trenton, NJ.

8   Kohnert, 'African migration to Europe', p. 8.

instead of the current 27).[9] Senegal being a Muslim country, it stands to reason that the African congregations in Europe are mainly founded by Christians from Ghana and Nigeria. Some ten years ago, these three first-ranking countries were followed by migrants from Cape Verde and Mali who, unlike those just mentioned, have mainly settled in one country, respectively Portugal and France (although The Netherlands have long had a stable Cape Verdean community in the port-city of Rotterdam. This Cape Verdean community is traditionally Catholic but has recently turned towards more charismatic forms of Christian belief). Côte d'Ivoire, the next country on the list, was traditionally an immigration country for other West Africans, and not a place from which people emigrated to Europe. This was caused only by the economic crisis that affected the country from the late 1980s. Together, these six are the most important countries in West Africa from which people have been migrating in recent times to Europe for economic reasons. They are followed by other countries in the region that have recently been affected by economic or political crises, Liberia and Sierra Leone being obvious examples. Other West African countries such as Benin, Niger and Burkina Faso make the smallest contribution to European immigration but, on the other hand, are among the most important producers of migrants in their own sub-region.

This is how the situation was more than a decade ago. There appear to be no significant changes in migration patterns from Africa, since West Africa remains the most prominent place in sub-Saharan Africa from where young Africans try to make their way to Europe, whose relative economic prosperity and political stability continue to exercise a considerable pull effect.[10] Thousands of young Africans have tried in recent years to cross the sea from the West African coasts of Senegal or Mauritania in extremely unsafe conditions to reach the

---

9   Ter Haar, *Halfway to Paradise*, pp. 128-32.

10 Eurostat Yearbook 2005, http://epp.eurostat.ec.europa.eu/, p. 73. According to the same source, 4 member states - Spain, Italy, Germany and the U.K. - together accounted for 83 % of the net inflow of all migrants into the EU-25 member states in 2003 (p.74). The 10 countries that joined the EU in 2004 generally experienced much lower rates of net migration (p.76). This has to be considered in view of the fact that, in 2004, Germany had the largest population within the 25 countries with more than 18 % of the total, followed by France, the U.K. and Italy with roughly 13% each. These four countries comprise 57% of the total population of today's European Union (p. 62-4).

Canary Islands, the bit of European territory that is closest to the West African coast. Many have paid with their lives as they have drowned on the way, often in view of the promised land. Pictures of Africans washing up alive or dead on the shores of southern Europe with their celebrated holiday resorts have gone around the world, as have the desperate attempts of many who have not yet made it that far to overcome the physical barriers surrounding the European enclaves of Ceuta and Melilla in North Africa. According to estimates by the Red Cross some 3,000 'boat refugees' have lost their lives over the past three years in their efforts to reach Europe. This has to be put in the perspective of an estimated total of 25,000 people who tried their luck in the year 2006, and the record of September of that same year when in one weekend 1,400 Africans safely reached the Canaries.[11] Estimates from the Spanish government are even higher, but all figures clearly indicate the huge loss of life involved. The average price of the risky crossing amounts to some 13,000 euros (This sum, incidentally, is also the average amount paid by Ghanaians in the Netherlands to a potential marriage partner with legal documents. Many of the African labour migrants are undocumented, that is they have no documents that allow them to live and work legally in the country of their stay. This is the case in all countries of Europe). The majority of these boat people are now coming from Senegal, Mauritania and Mali, which are predominantly Muslim countries. Previously, African migrants tried to leave from North Africa to reach the southern tip of Spain, with Gibraltar being close in sight, or one of the small islands off the Italian coast, such as Lampedusa. With these destinations having become more difficult to reach, due to stricter controls, new ones are being explored, including Malta, for example. Many prospective migrants have been pushed even further south down the coast of West Africa, into The Gambia and Guinea Bissau, from where they continue to try and reach European territory.

Many of the successful migrants find temporary work in Spain or Italy, both countries that need cheap seasonal labour. This is why Spain, for example, against the wish of other EU countries, has occasionally legalised the presence of labour migrants, including Africans, most recently in 2005 when no less than 70,000 undocumented migrants were provided with a residence permit. The

---

11 *NRC Handelsblad*, 2-3 December 2006, p. 38.

Spanish economy benefits from migration, legal or illegal. Immigrants to Spain are estimated to contribute 0.6 per cent of the Gross National Product (GNP). In contrast to southern Europe, northern European countries are not so much in need of cheap seasonal labour for which no special training is needed, but, rather, need more educated people who can fill the labour gap that is emerging due to the ageing of their population.[12] Border patrols and other policy measures, although they have had a certain effect, have not put a halt to migration, and are unlikely to do so in future. It is worth noting in this context the indispensable contribution immigrants make to the economy of their countries of origin: in 2005 the total sum of remittances of all migrants amounted to 232 billion US dollars, which is three to four times as much as the total sum spent on development aid in the world annually.[13] If we apply this to Ghana, for example, it appears that, according to the Bank of Ghana, in one year (2003) one billion U.S. dollars were remitted by Ghanaian migrants worldwide, or 15 per cent of Ghana's GNP.[14]

The unstoppable migration trend from Africa, and its consequences, have caused the European Union - through the European Commission - to establish so-called migration centres in the countries of origin.[15] The first one, which is in the process of being founded in Mali, will be a pilot project. If it is judged a success the experiment will be repeated in Senegal and Mauritania. The main objective is to discourage young African men and women from leaving for Europe illegally and help them find a job in their own countries. Others will be selected according to still unknown criteria to serve the European economies, either through temporary jobs for manual workers or through a 'blue-card' system for highly educated people. Whatever the end result, economic motives are likely to change European migration policies concerning Africa.

This, by and large, is the background against which the African Christian presence in Europe must be considered. Without this unforeseen mass migration from Africa, the current Christian mission

---

12 *Onze Wereld*, April 2007, jrg. 50, no. 4, p. 21.

13 *Internationale Samenwerking IS*, no. 7, September 2006, p. 15.

14 Ibid., no. 2 , March 2007, p. 39.

15 *Onze Wereld*, April 2007, pp.19-20.

from Africa would not have developed as it is doing today. It is entirely due to the late-twentieth century migration trend that Ghanaian and Nigerian labour migrants in particular, accompanied in substantial numbers by refugee migrants from notably Congo and Angola but also other West- and Central African countries, have infused Europe with a new spiritual ethos. They have taken the lead in founding new churches in all the countries where they have arrived. Not only have they founded new churches, they have also opened new shops, new enterprises, and established new media outlets, both locally or as part of a global network. They have initiated, and participate in, development programmes in their countries of origin, either through the numerous cultural associations that flourish among African immigrants or through the churches that regularly collect money for social programmes 'back home'.

Mission and migration

The close connection between mission and migration is widely acknowledged in mission studies, where it is traced back to the Bible. I may refer here in particular to Andrew Walls, who has written extensively about the diaspora factor in Christian history, drawing attention to migration as a biblical theme.[16] He distinguishes two types of migration that are of a punitive or redemptive nature respectively, dubbed 'Adamic' and 'Abrahamic' migration, both of which recur in the Bible in various ways and forms. The first type, punitive migration, is represented, among others, by the expulsion of Adam and Eve from paradise, Jacob's flight, or Joseph's forced stay in Egypt. Here, migration is the result of some sort of wrongdoing, leading to dislocation and deprivation. Migration thus stands for dispossession and the loss of place. Punitive migration, we may say, is a type of forced migration, which contrasts with the second type, that of redemptive migration. Although in the latter case there is also the reality of dislocation and loss of home, this is not the result of any wrongdoing. Abraham, who is considered the archetype of redemptive migration, is not expelled but divinely *called* from his city and promised a better future. His migration resembles much more a type of voluntary migration, which leaves the final decision with the

---

16 See notably Andrew Walls, 'Mission and migration: the diaspora factor in Christian history', *Journal of African Christian Thought*, vol. 5, no. 2, December 2002, pp. 3-12.

migrant himself. Hence, there are two sides to migration, which are not mutually exclusive and may show a certain overlap, but that symbolise opposite fates: disaster, on the one hand, and high promise, on the other. Migration, thus, as Andrew Walls explains, is not by definition something that furthers the Christian mission; it may also obstruct it. This principle equally applies to African Christians' mission in Europe, whose outcome and results cannot yet be predicted.

The important point to be drawn from this discussion is the awareness that migration, of various sorts, has been vital to the spread of Christianity throughout history. In the history of African migration we can easily see today how the forced migration of Africans through the transatlantic slave trade has left its religious traces on the Americas and influenced the Christian-religious landscape of North America in particular. For the time being we lack the historical distance to evaluate the possible effects of African labour migration on Europe, which is generally seen as voluntary migration. Forced and voluntary migration, however, often overlap, in ways not dissimilar to the relative distinction made by Walls between punitive and redemptive forms of migration. Both refugees and labour migrants who come to Europe can be said only to do so of their own free will to a limited degree, as they are driven by the political and economic conditions at home. Their migration may feel to them like a punitive migration, the type of migration that stands for disaster. It seems as if they are punished for a wrongdoing, but in this case one which is not of their own making. In effect, however, the migration may also be experienced as redemptive, as it holds the promise of a better future.

Part of that better future, many African Christians have soon come to realise, is to live in a Europe that knows about God rather than rejecting and abandoning him, as they believe West-Europeans in particular have done on a large scale. Although their analysis of secular Europe, frequently likened to a spiritual desert, often lacks conceptual depth, their first-hand experiences teach them that Europe needs re-evangelisation, and that this should be done by those who originally received the gospel from Europe. With reference to the prophet Ezekiel's vision of the valley of dry bones,[17] many African Christians believe that Europe can come back to spiritual life only if

---

17 Ezekiel 37, vs 1-15.

somebody will prophesy and tell the dry bones to listen to the word of God. In one of the African-initiated churches in the Netherlands, the United Assemblies of God International, this image has been developed into a mission programme under the title 'The Valley Vision'. Another church, the Church of Pentecost, expresses a similar view in its mission report, claiming that the reputation of the Christian churches in the Netherlands suffers from the 'deadening traditionalism, formalism, and theological disputes' which are hampering the missionary task.[18]

So, what we see today is that many African Christians who have recently migrated to Europe, generally to find work, consider that God has given them a unique opportunity to spread the good news among those who have gone astray. This ambition forms part of their church vision as recorded in their mission statement. The evangelising zeal is also clear from the stated aims and objectives of some of their mission organisations, such as the association called GATE, which originally stood for the Gospel from Africa To Europe, but was later changed into Gift from Africa To Europe.[19] In Belgium, African Christians created an organisation called DAWN, meaning 'Discipling A Whole Nation'.[20] These acronyms are expressive metaphors for the change of life which they hope to bring about. Whether or not their target audience appreciates it, a reverse mission is in progress, upsetting the conventional codes that have long prescribed that Africans ought to be on the receiving end, and Europeans on the giving one, of the relationship.

Yet, although changed in scope and character, the reverse mission trend is not entirely new, nor is it the sole invention of the Pentecostal or charismatic churches, as is often suggested. The Nigerian scholar Ogbu Kalu has traced the history of what he calls the 'reverse flow' in African Christianity and located its origins in the historic mainline churches in the nineteenth century, when some people foresaw a 'blessed reflex' in which the Western mission churches would be

---

18 *Know Your Mission Areas: The Church of Pentecost International Missions*, Accra: Pentecost Press, n.d, p. 41.

19 This was apparently under influence of those Dutch people who disliked the use of the original term.

20 See K. Cornil, 'La Nouvelle Jérusalem: bespreking van een Afrikaanse kerk-gemeenschap in Brussel', M.A thesis, Katholieke Universiteit Leuven, 1997, pp. 10-11.

challenged and renewed by the new churches springing up in Africa, Asia and Latin America.[21] He goes on to show how the terminology of 'blessed reflex' was reinvented as 'reverse flow' in missiological discourse in Africa during the late 1970s, as part of the debate on indigenisation, moratorium and the decolonisation of the church in Africa. The moratorium debate of the early 1970s, in particular, is of interest here, since part of that debate was about the question whether white Christians had a monopoly of cross-cultural mission. However, the early attempts to post African clergymen in Europe remained unsuccessful because, as Kalu puts it, '[t]hey were like visitors doing field placement in white churches'.[22] An additional difficulty was the problem of racism, which continues to affect relations between black and white Christians in Europe today.[23] Hence, independent African congregations emerged that managed to organise themselves successfully in Europe, at that time almost exclusively in Britain.[24]

This early picture has changed dramatically since the 1980s. Since then, largely as a result of African migration to Europe, the dynamics of African Christianity can no longer be denied, in spite of the numerous problems it encounters on the way, restrictive European immigration policies being the most obvious. Another obstacle is the housing problem. Many African-initiated churches in Europe lack a proper place to worship and have to seek temporary refuge in places not intended for that purpose. This not only contributes to their relative invisibility but also hampers their full development and functioning, including their missionary tasks. In The Netherlands, the problem is particularly acute in Amsterdam, where the largest number of migrant churches can be found, concentrated in the southeast district that is generally known as the 'Bijlmer'. In this district alone, at least 90 migrant churches were identified in 2005, the majority being

---

21 Ogbu U. Kalu, 'Anatomy of reverse flow in African Christianity: Pentecostalism and immigrant African Christianity', paper presented at the conference African Christianity and the Neo-Diaspora, St. Paul, Minnesota, March 23-25th, 2007.

22 Ibid.

23 See also Gerrie ter Haar, *Halfway to Paradise*, notably pp. 159-67.

24 For an early history of this process, see Hermione Harris, *Yoruba in Diaspora: An African Church in London*, New York and Basingstoke: Palgrave Macmillan, 2006.

African-initiated and mostly founded by Ghanaians.[25] To put this in wider perspective: in a small country like the Netherlands, throughout the country church services take place today in almost 90 different languages.[26] It suggests that we are getting no more than a glimpse of contemporary African religious dynamics in Europe.

At the time of my own research, some fifteen years ago, most of these churches had originally been founded independently from any other institution. They could be described as the by-product of migration, as they had emerged entirely from the migrant situation of African Christians in Europe. Only later would a formal link be established with one or another church in the country of origin, mostly Ghana and Nigeria, the pioneering countries in African church formation in Europe in the late-twentieth century. Only some African Christians would join an existing European church since, other than in Britain or France and quite apart from any other factors, the unfamiliar language often posed a serious problem and the ability to learn the new language was affected by the migrants' situation. In the course of time, much of this has changed. Nowadays church services are often held in several languages. Significantly, church services in the Netherlands have gradually moved from the predominant use of an African language in combination with English to a greater use of Dutch in combination with English, which is also the result of generational changes.

Theologically, there is an even greater barrier preventing Africans from joining European congregations. African Christianity has a number of characteristics that differ from mainstream Christianity in Europe. African Christians generally believe in a spirit world and in the power that may be derived from it: hence the importance of the Holy Spirit. They also tend to believe in the reality and presence of spiritual evil, also in the form of evil spirits or witchcraft. Hence, religious or ritual healing is a prominent feature of most of the churches, including deliverance. This emphasises the holistic nature of their ministry, in which material and immaterial wellbeing represent

---

25 See A.P. van den Broek, 'Ieder Hoorde in zijn Eigen Taal: Inventarisatie van Kerken voor – en van – Nieuwkomers en Migranten in Nederland', Amstelveen, February 2005. (Privately produced).

26 Ibid.

two sides of the same coin. Unlike European churches, most of the African-initiated churches are charismatic in nature. They are spirit-oriented and evangelical in character, basing themselves strongly on the Bible, and they are overtly and self-confidently missionary. They have often been formed on the basis of a personal vocation, which is one reason why there are so many independent congregations. The divine call cannot be resisted, as 'God's yes was louder than my no',[27] a well-known feature of African religious history. As part of the vocation, the one who is called is charged with a mission. Typically, this includes the task to go out and preach the gospel, or: to evangelise. As one pastor in the Bijlmer district, where I conducted my main research, expressed it: 'Jesus did not say: "come and stand beside me". He said: "Follow me".' It is a statement that can be seen as a short summary of both the dynamics and missionary engagement of African Christianity.[28]

The missionary engagement of African Christians is not limited to Europe. Since Africans have migrated to all parts of the world in recent decades, they have founded churches all over the globe. Today, many African-initiated churches in Europe have either become branches of existing churches in Africa or have been deliberately planted as such. Well-known examples include the Redeemed Christian Church of God, which has its headquarters in Nigeria, and the Church of Pentecost, which has its headquarters in Ghana. These are well-developed churches which have all the resources they need - material and spiritual - to implement a careful mission strategy that today also includes Europe.[29] The RCCG, for example, states as its explicit aim that it wants to plant churches within five minutes' walking distance in every city and town of developing countries, and within five minutes driving distance in every city or town of developed countries.[30] Or, adapted to American circumstances, within 30

---

27 W.H. Myers, *God's Yes was Louder than my No: Rethinking the African-American Call to Ministry*, Grand Rapids: W.B. Eerdmans, 1994.

28 Personal interview with Rev. Daniel Himmans-Arday of the True Teachings of Christ's Temple, Amsterdam-Zuidoost, 17 May 2007.

29 For a full-length study of the Redeemed Christian Church of God, see Ukah, *A New Paradigm of Pentecostal Power*.

30 See the church's mission statement at the RCCG website www.rccg.org.

minutes' driving distance,[31] an aim which has proven to be not only rhetorical, as RCCG branches have been established in about 60 countries, with over two million proclaimed members. For a country such as The Netherlands, the church's vision has been equally adapted to local circumstances, in this case 'to have a fellowship venue (be it a church hall or other meeting place) within a 30-minute commuting distance from where you live'.[32] This is just one example, but there are many more African mega-churches with active evangelisation policies. While in western and northern Europe the ultimate aim is spiritual renewal, in Eastern Europe it often means converting people. An exceptional example comes from Nigeria again. This concerns The Embassy of the Blessed Kingdom of God for All Nations, a church that was founded in Ukraine in the early 1990s by a former African student in Russia, the Nigerian Sunday Adelaja. According to the Ghanaian scholar Kwabena Asamoah-Gyadu, 90% of the 20,000 adult members are, quite untypically, indigenous Europeans.[33] The church has spread to many other countries, in and outside Europe, mostly in Eastern Europe. Its ultimate ambition, according to its founder, is to effect another reformation.[34]

But, as Ogbu Kalu also reminds us, a focus on these few successful mega-churches should not blind us to the fact that the majority of African-initiated churches in Europe are struggling to survive.[35] Not only do they often lack a proper place to worship, in many cases they also have very limited financial resources, raised from members with no or low-paid jobs, many of whom have enormous social problems inherent to their immigrant status. Illness, depression, marital problems, lack of job and education facilities, language problems, and so on: the list is virtually endless. No surprise, then, that many churches are fully preoccupied with keeping their own flock together,

---

31 Ibid. See also Afe Adogame, 'Contesting the ambivalences of modernity in a global context: The Redeemed Christian Church of God, North America', *Studies in World Christianity*, vol, 10, part 1, 2004, pp. 25-48, notably at p. 32.

32 <www.rccgholland.org>.

33 J. Kwabena Asamoah-Gyadu, 'African-initiated Christianity in eastern Europe: Church of the "Embassy of God" in Ukraine', *International Bulletin of Missionary Research*, vol. 30, no. 2, 2006, pp. 73-5.

34 See the church's website at www.godembassy.org.

35 Kalu, 'Anatomy of reverse flow'. See also Ter Haar, *Halfway to Paradise*.

before they can reach out to others. Hence, those in charge of a congregation often have limited time and opportunity to evangelise outside their own circle. This is where the phenomenon of African itinerant preachers comes in, a model with which contemporary European churches are usually unfamiliar. Yet, there appear to be plenty of these, individuals with a vocation, who link up with a particular congregation but consider their main task as that of evangelisation. In effect they seem to conform most closely to the Macedonian model of migration that Jehu Hanciles has proposed in addition to the Adamic and Abrahamic distinction made by Andrew Walls.[36] This model is based on the request from Macedonia that came to Paul in a vision, as recorded in the Acts of the apostles, 'to come over and help'.[37] Hence, Hanciles suggests, it 'embodies planned or structured official initiatives or responses, typically involving institutions acting on a conviction that God has called them to proclaim the gospel in a particular place'.[38] Although the original vocation of the itinerant pastor most resembles the Abrahamic model, in its elaboration it comes closer to the Macedonian one, as the itinerant nature of their ministry allows these pastors to engage in missionary outreach in ways their congregation-bound counterparts often cannot. Itinerant preachers are normally not represented in mission statistics, nor are those who run home congregations or other types of fellowship, or the pastors of the numerous small-scale churches, with no more than 50 members or even less, who do not belong to any recognised or recognisable larger structure but nevertheless may be assumed to represent many African Christians in Europe. It is part of the relative invisibility that goes with migrant status and which has to be distinguished from those churches that have been consciously planted as part of a missionary strategy initiated from Africa (such as the RCCG).

The marginal status of many migrant churches also obscures the contribution they make to society as a whole. In 2006, the organisation

---

36 Jehu J. Hanciles, 'Beyond Christendom: African migration and transformations in global Christianity', *Studies in World Christianity*, vol. 10, part 1, 2004, 93-113.

37 Acts 16, vs. 9.

38 Hanciles, 'Beyond Christendom', p. 104.

of migrant churches in the Netherlands, called SKIN,[39] commissioned an investigation with regard to churches in The Hague.[40] Half of the sample concerned African-initiated churches. To investigate the social gain represented by the churches, the researchers used a method based on the American concept of Social Return On Investment (SROI), by which the value of voluntary work is expressed in monetary terms. Hence, they looked at the costs that are saved by the rest of society (government, business, non-profit organisations) as a result of the social activities of the churches, or: the costs that society as a whole saves because a specific social group performs certain tasks for free.[41] Examples are: psycho-social care, not only for members but also including others, practical social work, policy work, education and training, youth activities, cultural activities, as well as missionary activities. In The Hague, these include: introduction courses about the Christian faith, so-called 'prayer posts', where people pray with others in the street, the house-to-house distribution of Christian pamphlets as a way of evangelising, local radio and TV broadcasts, and addressing people in public. It appears that the sample churches in The Hague spend annually 18,000 hours on missionary activities which, in financial terms, amounts to more than 554,000 euros.[42] Only part of these activities are translatable into social gain, for example in the case of visits to the homeless or to prostitutes, local radio or television programmes with an informative character, or courses with a general orientation.[43] The question of what missionary activities are was also discussed in the churches that were part of the survey. Most often these were considered as all those activities that aim to convince others to become Christian. But there also existed the additional idea that evangelisation is not just a matter of words, but rather of deeds. Or, as the pastor of one of the Bijlmer churches once expressed it: 'Mission

---

39 A Dutch acronym that stands for Samen Kerk in Nederland (Together Church in The Netherlands), but at the same time conveys the message of the continuing importance of race relations in the churches.

40 Jaap van der Sar and Roos Visser, 'Gratis en Waardevol: Rol, Positie en Maatschappelijk Rendement van Migrantenkerken in Den Haag', Stichting Oikos, 2006.

41 Ibid., p. 31.

42 The total social gain of migrant churches in The Hague was estimated at more than 17.5 million euro.

43 Van der Sar and Visser, p. 23.

is about making a difference. It is important to be an example. A good example contaminates. When your presence makes a difference, you are into something good'.[44] In order for these new churches to increase their social benefit, the state will have to change its attitude towards them. Most of all, it must create the conditions for them to carry out their work. In other words, a re-thinking of the relation between church and state is needed, a point that was also made in the SKIN report mentioned.

These new mission dynamics are not adequately reflected in the statistics compiled every year by David Barrett et al., as their 'missiometrics' are based on established structures.[45] That is, they refer to personnel employed full-time by churches and mission agencies, also including desk officers and so on. What they do show, however, is that Africa, too, has become a sending continent, even though it continues to receive far more foreign missionaries than it is itself sending out. According to the latest statistics from this source, published in 2007, almost 18,500 African citizens work as mission personnel outside their own continent. This includes not only Europe, as African missionaries can be found in all continents today. Although according to these conventional statistics Africa's sending power is still far below that of Europe (more than 203,000 mission personnel sent), it is interesting to see that these same statistics indicate that Europe today receives more missionaries from abroad (not only from Africa) than does Africa: almost 112,000 against almost 96,000.[46] For the reasons I have mentioned, these 'official' statistical data have to be viewed with a fair degree of scepticism. There is one further fact emerging from these statistics that is worth mentioning in this context, as it specifically affects the relationship between Africa and Europe. Among the eleven countries that send out the largest number of missionaries - that is, over 10,000 each - are seven European ones. Four of these - Britain, France, Germany and Italy - are also receiving the largest number of foreign missionaries (over 10,000 each). They are also among the countries with the greatest African Christian

---

44 Personal interview with Rev. Daniel Himmans-Arday, 17 May 2007.

45 David B. Barrett, Todd M. Johnson, and Peter F. Crossing, 'Missiometrics 2007: Creating your own analysis of global data', *International Bulletin of Missionary Research*, vol. 31, nr. 1, Jan. 2007, pp. 25-32.

46 The exact figures are: 111,828 and 95,765.

presence. If, as projected, Africa will indeed grow into the continent with the largest Christian presence by the year 2025, this is bound to affect any accurate statistics on global mission. In that case too, African mission will continue to be not exclusively the result of a careful mission plan, but considered to be the result of the discretion of the Holy Spirit.[47]

New realities, new meanings?

The cold reception that many Africans initially experienced on their arrival in Europe caused the black majority churches in Britain to direct their missionary activities in the first instance towards their fellow-Africans rather than towards the indigenous population, as Patrick Kalilombe, former director of the Centre for Black and White Christian Partnership in Birmingham, has noted. The origins of black Christianity in Britain, according to him, lie in the work of pastors and preachers of Afro-Caribbean origin who went out into the streets to look for 'those who were in need and call[ed] out to them that there was hope'.[48] In light of this history, we may appreciate that the valley of dry bones is more than a biblical phrase used by some African preachers to describe the spiritual condition of Europe. It is also a metaphor for the cold reception which often awaits African immigrants on their arrival. This theme is common to many of the stories told by Africans about life in Europe. In Britain the unfriendly reception accorded to black immigrants by the established churches forty or fifty years ago was the immediate reason for Africans and Afro-Caribbeans to found independent churches in this particular country.

The same now appears to be happening in continental Europe, where the African-initiated churches seem to minister primarily to a black, African constituency. This has provoked many Western observers to consider these churches as 'ethnic' churches, whose stated ambition of being an 'international' church, open to all races, is far beyond reality, and, one suspects, should better remain a figment of the religious imagination. I have repeatedly argued that such a view is

---

47 Personal interview with Rev. Daniel Himmans-Arday, 17 May 2007.

48 Patrick Kalilombe, 'Black Christianity in Britain and its missionary outreach'. Paper presented at the Ethnic and Racial Studies Conference on 'Ethnic Minorities and Religion', London School of Economics, 12 May, 1995.

unreasonable, uninformed and unjustified. African Christians in Europe themselves do not consider their churches as 'African' churches but, as the names of their congregations almost invariably indicate, as 'international' churches, expressing their aspiration to be part of the international world in which they believe themselves to have a universal task. I have suggested, therefore, that it would be more appropriate to refer to the African-initiated churches in Europe today as African *international* churches, a term which does justice to both the subjective perspective of the insider who has chosen this term, and the objective view of the outsider who cannot ignore the international distribution of these churches today. As African International Churches these congregations represent the latest phase in the African church movement that became historically known under the acronym AIC (African Independent Churches). It is an appellation that does justice to the historical significance of these churches in a globalised world, while at the same time showing their continuity with the past by providing the well-known abbreviation of AIC with new meaning.[49]

In a similar vein, I would like to argue that the academic preference to refer to the current process of international migration as *trans*migration and to international migrants as *trans*migrants betrays a similar type of reasoning. In such a view, African migrants are seen as moving between the borders of two countries: their country of origin and their new country of settlement. They are seen as people who move between the borders of these two countries and cultures, in both of which they participate and between which they provide a helpful link.[50] Although the link with the country of origin remains significant and important, certainly among many first-generation immigrants, such

---

49 Originally known as African independent churches or, in short AIC's, the content of the 'I'-initial has been subject to change ever since these churches emerged in Africa in the late nineteenth and early twentieth centuries. Apart from African 'independent' churches, these churches have been labelled over time as African 'indigenous', African 'instituted', and African 'initiated' churches. The change of appellation is a telling illustration of the change of perspective it implies concerning a historic phenomenon at different points of time. The rise of African congregations in the Netherlands and other parts of the European continent reflects yet another change of perspective which can best be expressed by the term African 'international' churches.

50 Cf. Hanciles, 'Beyond Christendom', p. 98. See also Ibid., 'Mission and migration: some implications for the twenty-first-century church', *International Bulletin of Missionary Research*, vol. 27, no. 4, pp. 146-53, esp. p. 148.

an image ignores one of the most remarkable characteristics of modern African migration, namely that contemporary migrants move between multiple borders, creating links between migrants in all parts of the world and thus creating new and rather more complex networks. The network character of migration is typical of late-twentieth century migration as facilitated by modern technology and mass communication. It is likely to become even more so in the twenty-first century. This fact alone cries out for an academic approach that does not study African Christians in Europe only in relation to their original homelands,[51] but in regard to the networks they create all over the world, in this case notably in Europe. These may include Africans and non-Africans, such as, for example, in the global Pentecostal movement that binds many non-Western Christians together. European Christians are often unaware of these dynamics, while Western scholars appear uninterested in researching them as they remain preoccupied with the idea that Africans 'really' belong in Africa. In the present era, however, African-initiated churches are no longer territorially bounded.

One of the problems that Western observers are struggling with in grasping unfamiliar realities, I have noted elsewhere, is in the use of their analytical categories, which are often derived from their own history.[52] A similar point is made by Jehu Hanciles, a scholar from Sierra Leone residing in the United States, when commenting on the effects of African Christian migration to the United States.[53] In both cases, whether it concerns Europe or America, there is an urgent need for developing new conceptual tools to understand the reverse mission in progress. This also implies, as Hanciles notes, a need for new missiological perspectives, 'not least because the missionary movement emerging out of non-Western societies is framed by radically different understandings and assumptions from those which characterised the earlier Western missionary movement.'[54] It is undoubtedly true, as he concludes, that the dominance of Western

---

51 This appears to be an approach especially favoured by Western anthropologists studying this new development.

52 See Stephen Ellis and Gerrie ter Haar, *Worlds of Power: Religious Thought and Political Practice in Africa*, London: C. Hurst & Co., notably ch. 1.

53 Hanciles, 'Beyond Christendom'.

54 Ibid., p. 100.

scholarship is to a large extent responsible for this problem, by projecting Western concepts and theoretical assumptions onto new realities, 'distorting images and befogging understanding.'[55] It is also true, however, that too many African scholars seem to feel beholden to dominant models of Western scholarship, something that a younger generation of scholars from Africa appears to be less burdened with, as some recent works from Africa testify.[56] This is part of what one might call the 'decolonisation of the mind', one of the last phases in the decolonisation process worldwide, in which the religious realities of the majority of peoples in the world are bound to play a role.[57]

The problem posed to Western scholarship of how to deal conceptually with new realities also concerns the concept of 'migrant church' that is normally used to describe the churches under discussion. Although the migrant status, as I have consistently argued, is vital to the life of many of these churches, this label causes a series of problems. Not only, as is so often the case with labelling, does the name reflect the dominant perspective of the host country, but it also runs the risk of turning their migrant origin into a permanent status. Moreover, it further obscures their self-identification as international churches, while at the same time effectively restricting their possibility to reach out to non-Africans. The message contained in the label seems to affirm that these are churches by and for a particular group of people, who hold a marginal position in society. The point has also to be considered in the context of the political climate in Europe, that is generally anti-foreigner and anti-migration. Migrants are outsiders, and the terminology used confirms that position. The continuous use of special labels - such as 'African churches' or 'migrant churches' - to refer to the new churches in Europe helps to maintain an image of otherness and confirms their temporary status. Many members of these churches, however, do not want to refer to themselves as 'migrants'. They consider themselves as Christians, albeit with a particular ethnic or cultural background – i.e. African - who want to

---

55 Ibid. Also Ellis and Ter Haar, *Worlds of Power*, ch. 1.

56 Recent examples include Matthews A. Ojo, *The End-Time Army: Charismatic Movements in Modern Nigeria* (Trenton, NJ: Africa World Press, 2006), and Ukah's *A New Paradigm of Pentecostal Power*. Both monographs, published in the newly established series 'Religion in Contemporary Africa', discuss the new religious dynamism in Africa.

57 Ellis and Ter Haar, *Worlds of Power*, ch. 9.

make a lasting contribution to their new society. Hence, they do not emphasise cultural *differences* in the experiences of the Christian faith but its culture-transcending unity.

In the final chapter of *Halfway to Paradise* I argued that one of the recurring problems is to decide how to refer to people who have moved their place of residence from Africa to Europe.[58] Are they Africans who happen to live in Europe? Are they black Europeans? How long must a foreigner live in Europe to qualify as a European? These considerations apply not only to people but also to their ideas and their institutions. If we refer to a church established in Amsterdam by a person born in Ghana, and attended overwhelmingly by others from Africa, as an African church, it is to imply strongly that it is not for Europeans. If we refer to the faith which African immigrants profess when they are in Europe as African Christianity, it may equally imply that this is of a special ethnic brand, not for European use. What is of crucial importance, therefore, is the precise significance which is attached to these labels. In this respect the connotations attached in Europe to any label which has African written on it are powerful ones, summarising all the respects in which Africans are generally believed to be different from Europeans. Concepts of otherness, like all ideas, have a history, and in the case of Europe it is one which includes the experiences of colonialism and nineteenth-century missionary enterprise as well as ideas generated by media reports of more recent events, including famines and wars. All of this provides part of the ideological baggage which many Europeans carry with them and which they may unpack when they read a description of somebody or something as 'African'. This baggage is a legacy of the past, which cannot be relived. But in applying labels and descriptions today it seems important to be aware of the great speed with which Africa itself is changing and with which its links with other parts of the world are being re-forged, sometimes in surprising ways.

---

58 See Ter Haar, *Halfway to Paradise*, ch. 10.

52

Chapter Three

Nigerian Pentecostal Missionary enterprise in Kenya: Taking the Cross Over*

Philomena Mwaura

Scholars of world Christianity have underscored the shifting contours of the Christian religion.[1] In the 20th century, a diminishing of Christianity in its former bastions in the northern continents and a corresponding shift of its centre of gravity in the south has been witnessed. The growth of Christianity in Africa has been so tremendous that according to the *World Christian Encyclopaedia*, the Christian population grew from 9.9 million in 1900 to 360 million in 2000.[2] Barrett et al further observed that 'the present net increase on the continent is 8.4 million Christians a year (23,000 a day) of which 1.5 million are new converts.'[3] This growth has been attributed not only to the impetus of the modern missionary movement, but also the tireless toil, determination and evangelistic fervours of local agency, especially clergy, catechists and lay people through proclamation and personal witness.

While contemporary migrant religiosity in Western Europe and North America has been arduously studied and much literature

---

* This paper is adapted from 'Nigerian Pentecostal Missionary Enterprise in Kenya', in Korie Chima and Ugo Nwokeji (eds), *Religion, History and Politics in Nigeria: Essays in Honour of Ogbu U. Kalu*, University of America Press, 2005.

1   See for example Phillip Jenkins, *The Next Christendom: The Coming of Global Christianity*, Oxford: Oxford University Press, 2002; Dana Roberts, 'Shifting Southward; Global Christianity since 1945', *International Bulletin of Missionary Research*, April 2000; Andrew F. Walls, *The Missionary Movement in Christian History*, New York: Mary Knoll Orbis Books, 2000.

2   David Barrett, George T. Kurian, and Todd M. Johnson, *World Christian Encyclopaedia: A Comparative Survey of Churches and Religions in the Modern World*, New York: Oxford University Press, 2001; 1:5.

3   Barret et al, *World Christian Encyclopaedia*.

generated, intra African mission has not received any significant attention. Yet charismatic churches and the older/classical African Independent Churches (AIC's) have been evangelising neighbouring countries and others far beyond. The phenomenon of West, East, Southern and Central African Charismatic churches planting churches cross regionally has escalated since the mid 1980's.

This chapter, therefore seeks to explore the development of Nigerian Pentecostal missionary enterprise in Kenya and assess its missiological implications for the growth and character of the church in Kenya. Although there are migrant churches in Kenya established by immigrants from the Democratic Republic of Congo, Ethiopia and Eritrea, these will not be dealt with in this chapter. They nevertheless require to be studied in order to establish their nature, characteristics, mission dynamics and functions for the migrants and within Kenyan Christianity.

The chapter also discusses some basic Pentecostal teachings, for example, salvation, deliverance theology and evangelism, especially as they relate to Nigerian Pentecostal mission. It is evident that since the 1980's, Nigerian Pentecostal preachers have been going to Kenya on evangelistic missions at the invitation of Kenyan Pentecostal pastors and some have ended up establishing churches in Nairobi and other parts of the country. The Nigerian brand of Pentecostalism has also permeated Kenyan Christianity through Nigerian Christian films, spiritual literature and audio and video tapes of sermons and music.

The question therefore arises, what motivates Nigerian pastors to go to Kenya? What theologies and practices of mission do they bring? Nigerian Pentecostal churches with branches in Kenya include Deeper Life Bible Church, Winners Chapel International, Christ Embassy, Victorious Faith Assembly and Redeemed Christian Church of God.

Literature on these churches in Kenya is virtually non existent. The author therefore relied on oral sources. The focus is on three churches namely, Redeemed Christian Church of God, Winners Chapel International and Victorious Faith Assembly.

Defining Nigerian Pentecostalism

Scholars of Nigerian Pentecostalism identify two major phases of revival within Nigerian Christianity which have led to the evolution of two distinct strands of churches. Matthew Ojo[4] distinguishes between Pentecostal and charismatic groups while Ruth Marshall[5] distinguishes between the holiness movement and the Pentecostals. The terms are confusing but seem to be based on the historical foundations of these movements and doctrinal emphasis. Ruth Marshall prefers to refer to the whole revival movement, regardless of periodisation, as 'born again'. To her the common denominator in the movement is the conversion experience of being 'born again' through individual acts of repentance and submission.

The holiness/Pentecostal churches have their roots in the student movement and fervent mission activity of the 1960s and 1970s. In structure and organisation they are close to their mother churches, that is, the classical Pentecostal churches introduced into Nigeria by American and British missionaries in the 1920s to 1950s. Their doctrinal stress is on perfection, strict personal ethics, biblical inerrancy, and a disdain for the 'world', interpreted as materialism and carnal pleasure which are viewed as sinful. They also emphasise personal salvation, baptism in the Holy Spirit, and speaking in tongues.

The charismatic or Pentecostals, as Marshall designates them have their roots in the revival within the holiness churches in the 1970s, 1980s, and 1990s. This revival gave birth to the trans-denominational charismatic groups with a base in universities and students' groups. The revival was fuelled by an influx of American Pentecostals through literature, radio, and television broadcasts, and personal visits to

---

4   Matthew Ojo, 'Deeper Life Bible Church of Nigeria', in *New Dimensions in African Christianity*, Paul Gifford (ed), Nairobi: All Africa Conference of Churches, 1992, 135-137.   See also Matthew Ojo, 'The Charismatic Movement in Nigeria Today', *International Bulletin of Missionary Research* 19 no. 3, 1995: 114-18; Matthew Ojo, 'Sexuality, Marriage and Piety Among Charismatics in Nigeria', *Rites of Passage in Contemporary Africa: Interaction Between Christian and African   Traditional Religions*, James Cox (ed), Cardiff: Academic Press 1998, 182-85.

5   Marshall, 'Pentecostalism in Southern Nigeria, An Overview', *New Dimensions in African Christianity,* Paul Gifford ed), Nairobi: All Africa Conference of Churches, 1992, 9-19.   See also Ruth Marshall '"God is not a Democrat" Pentecostalism and Democratization of Africa', in Paul Gifford (ed), *The Christian Churches and the Democratisation of Africa,* Leiden: E.J. Brill, 1995, 239-60.

Nigeria and elsewhere. Unlike the holiness churches, which were characterised by a retreatist attitude from the world, the charismatics adopted a faith gospel focused on worldly blessings and a deliverance theology. They have adopted a doctrine of prosperity 'in which the spiritual and material fortunes of a believer are dependent on how much he gives, spiritually and materially to God who will reward him by prospering him.' [6]

This revival has also been associated with the rise of the faith movement all over Africa which was influenced by American evangelism on the continent. Several African founders of charismatic churches have been trained or mentored by proponents of the faith and prosperity gospel such as Kenneth Hagin Sr. and John Avanzini. Such Nigerian leaders are Benson Idahosa of Church of God Mission, David Oyedepo of Winners' Chapel International, and Enoch A. Adeboye, General Overseer of Redeemed Christian Church of God (RCCG). Others such as Paul Aigboje of Victorious Faith Assembly were influenced by the writings of Myles Monroe, Derek Prince, Kenneth Hagin Sr., E.W. Kenyon and Joyce Meyer.

The charismatic churches have incorporated high percentage of educated, up-worldly mobile youth and a "charismatic" doctrine which stresses experiential faith, the centrality of the Holy Spirit, and the spiritual gifts of speaking in tongues, faith healing, miracles, and evangelism. Marshall points out that Nigerians label these churches as Pentecostal, despite the fact that the whole movement identifies itself as Pentecostal. In Ghana these churches speak of themselves as 'Charismatic Churches' or charismatic ministries.[7] In Kenya, the churches designate themselves as Pentecostal. Scholars of the phenomenon prefer to call them African Pentecostal churches to distinguish them from classical Pentecostal churches that were established at the beginning of the Twentieth century. 'Charismatic movement' is a term used to refer solely to the charismatic renewal within mainstream Christianity, whether Protestant or Catholic. In this chapter the preferred term is Pentecostal/charismatic.

---

6   Marshall, 'Pentecostalism in Southern Nigeria', 15.

7   Kwabena Asamoah-Gyadu, 'Fireballs in our Midst: West Africa's Burgeoning Charismatic Churches and the Pastoral Roles of Women', *Mission Studies* Vol 15-1 no. 2a, 19998, 15.

Foundations of Pentecostal/Charismatic Christianity in Kenya

When Nigerian Pentecostal missionaries established contact in Kenya, they found a ground that had already been prepared by classical Pentecostal missionaries from America and Canada and the East African Revival Movement. As early as the 1920s, revival had occurred in the Friends African Mission (Quakers) in Kaimosi, in the Pentecostal Assemblies of Canada mission in Nyang'ori, western Kenya, and in the Africa Inland Mission at Kijabe in central Kenya. The revival stressed personal salvation and the importance of receiving the Holy Spirit as a sign of sanctification. Confession of sins and speaking in tongues were later stressed by the African converts as evidence of receiving the Holy Spirit. The emergence of the revival was an African reaction to a Christianity that did not adequately address Africans' spiritual needs. This Pentecostal experience resulted in the emergence of AICs of the spiritual Zionist variety.[8]

The East African revival started in Rwanda and spread to Uganda, Kenya, and Tanzania. The revival, commonly referred to as the *Balokole* (saved ones in Luganda) or Ahonoki (saved ones in Gikuyu), evolved within missionary churches. Mark Winters defines the movement as a 'revival in which nominal or "backslidden" Christians are "revived" in their commitment to the faith; it is not primarily a movement of charismatisation affecting non-Christians.'[9] The movement was interdenominational, interracial, and interethnic. It was also a response to the perceived lethargy of missionary Christianity and its having been compromised to worldliness. It emphasised the experience of personal salvation through the blood of Jesus, personal holiness, asceticism, confessions of sins, hard work, and reliability. The *Balokole* Movement empowered the laity, literate and illiterate, to testify for Jesus. This had an impact in the evolution of patterns of ministry that were different from those of mainline churches.

In the 1960s and 1970s, American Evangelists such as Billy Graham and T.L. Osborne visited Kenya, and this helped the

---

8   William B. Anderson, *The Church in East Africa 1840-1974*, Nairobi: Uzima Press, 1977, 118-20.

9   Mark Winters, 'The Balokole and the Protestant Ethic: A Critique', *Journal of Religion in Africa* 14, no. 1, 1983, 69.

revivalists to discover that revival was a worldwide phenomenon and entailed more than preaching. It entailed other gifts such as healing. In schools and colleges revival was carried out by the Kenyan Students Christian Fellowship. University ministry had regular missions to the whole university every three years. A network of hall prayers and Bible study sessions were planned to enhance Christian nurture to the university student communities. In high schools and junior colleges, Christian Unions were organised to facilitate spiritual nurture through prayers and bible studies in each school or college. Camps were organised in key regional schools to train students on holistic spiritual growth. Leaders of the revival were generally lay men and women who had little theological formation, but they worked tirelessly to involve schools and colleges. Many lay people who were involved in the revival later became prominent personalities and even founded churches and parachurch organisations, for example Joe Kayo, founder of the Deliverance Church; David Kimani, founder of Bethel Mission; and Reverend Margaret Wangari, presiding bishop of the Church of the Lord. The churches they founded are dotted all over the country.

The crystallisation of the revival movement into churches is attributed not only to the charismatic nature of the preachers and their powerful and relevant messages that transcended barriers of gender, class, age, but also to the problem mainline churches found themselves in after Kenya's independence in 1963. They were mostly concerned with managing churches and developing their social ministries in education and health, and they lacked adequate personnel for pastoral work in schools and other educational institutions. These were years of transition, and Nigeria, as Ojo reports, had similar experience of revival.

From the 1980s to the present, Pentecostal fellowships, ministries, and churches have proliferated, some founded by the indigenous Kenyans and others founded by international evangelists from Europe, Asia, America, and other parts of Africa. Itinerant televangelists such as Reinhardt Bonke, Benny Hinn, Moriss Cerulo, Joyce Meyer, Cecil Stewart, Emmanuel Eni, and Simon Iheancho have graced the Kenyan capital of Nairobi and other major towns. As Mugambi observes, these personalities preside 'over personal enterprises not directly related to any specific denominations... they claim to have spiritual gifts and charismatic powers of preaching and faith healing.'[10] The emphasis in these campaigns has been a 'spiritual renewal' and numerical expansion of Christianity.

As with some other countries in the two-thirds world, Kenya has experienced the consequences of years of misrule and ineptitude, declining economy, corruption, environmental degradation, and the impact of Structural Adjustment Programs between 1988 and 2002. Gifford avers that the phenomenal growth of Christianity in Africa has risen in the context of economic decline, rising poverty, bad governance and international indifference.[11] It is into this social–religious background that Nigerian missionaries from Pentecostal churches have come. However, encounter between Kenyan and Nigerian Pentecostals predate the 1990s. Since the 1980s, they have collaborated in ministry in parachurch associations such as Full Gospel Businessmen's Fellowship and Women Aglow and shared platforms in crusades in both Nigeria and Kenya. As early as 1980, Bishop Margaret Wangare underwent a theological training course in Benin, Bendel State, Nigeria. While there, she was under the tutelage and guidance of the late Archbishop Benson Idahosa, founder of the Church of God Mission. Idahosa's influence was later to reach Kenya through the Winners' Chapel of David Oyedepo, Idahosa's former 'spiritual child'. This is one of the prominent Nigerian charismatic churches in Kenya. Emanuel Eni's literature, particularly his testimony in *Delivered from the Powers of Darkness* and his subsequent visit to Kenya in 1990 exposed Kenyans to the theology of power and deliverance. A number of people trace their disenchantment with mainline Christianity to the forceful evangelism and teachings delivered by these 'anointed men of God'. By the time the three churches that are the focus of this paper appeared on the scene, Nigerian Pentecostalism was not a novel phenomenon, and it benefited from previous experiences of revival in the church in Kenya.

---

10 Jesse N.K. Mugambi, 'Evangelistic and Charismatic Initiatives in Post Colonial Africa,' *Charismatic Renewal in Africa: A Challenge for African Christianity,* ed. Mika Vahakangas and Andrew A. Kyomo, Nairobi: Action Publishers 2003, 121.

11 Paul Gifford, 'Introduction', *The Christian Churches and the Democratization of Africa,* 5.

The Redeemed Christian Church of God

The Redeemed Christian Church of God (RCCG) is currently described as one of the fastest growing Pentecostal denominations in Nigeria. It was founded in 1952 by Josiah Akindayomi Olufemi, a Yoruba preacher from western Nigeria. The expansion of the church today is attributed to the current General Overseer, Enoch Adegboye, who took over the leadership when Akindayomi died in 1980. At that time the RCCG had only a few churches. Under Adegboye it has grown to five thousand congregations and an estimated three million adherents in Nigeria alone.[12] The church views its mission as primarily evangelical.[13] In fact, Adegboye sees a divine strategy behind the Pentecostal boom in Nigeria. He says 'perhaps God is rising up an authority to evangelise all Africa from here.'[14] It is alleged that RCCG, for example starts three new churches in Nigeria every day.[15]

The most important trait of Nigerian revival is that it is not confined to Nigeria. The RCCG, for example, started a Kenyan branch in 1995. Their first point of contact in Kenya was through a Kenyan lady, Elizabeth Okiniyi, married to a Nigerian and living in Lagos, who was a member of RCCG. Through Okiniyi, the RCCG sought ways of establishing a missionary outpost in Kenya. On 21 October 1995, Pastor Prince Okechukwu Obasi-ike and Pastor Ademila Farimu arrived in Nairobi and were hosted by Okiniyi's brother, Lester Wako, and his wife Gladys Wako. The church began in their home with counselling, prayer, deliverance and bible study. It later moved to the Young Men's Christian Association, South C Hostel.[16] The congregation then had a core of six people, namely two Nigerian pastors, Lester and Gladys, Benard Ndakwa, and Mary Wanalo. Another member was Richard Oba, a Ugandan then staying at the hostel. He was instrumental in setting up the RCCG in Uganda.

---

12 J. Lee Grady, 'Nigerian Miracle', *Charisma* 27, no. 10, May 2002, 42.

13 *The Redeemed Voice*, 'AGO Outlines, RCCG Doctrines and Teachings', *Moving On Higher Ground*, November 1998, 8.

14 Grady 'Nigerian Miracle', 42.

15 Ibid.

16 Oral interview Pastor Benson Kondia, Nairobi, 11 February, 2003.

The congregation grew steadily and soon moved to the Kenya Medical Association (KMA) Estate, South C. A sanctuary was later built there and it was dedicated by the General Overseer, Enoch Adegboye, in March 1966. Finally the RCCG purchased its own premises on Kirichwa Road, Milimani. Here they have a temporary worship sanctuary and a bible School where training for missions to unreached parts of the East African region is done. The place is also the Head quarters of the church in the East African region, covering Rwanda, Tanzania, Uganda, Ethiopia, Somalia, Burundi, and Djibouti. According to Pastor Benson Mwangi Kondia, the RCCG emphasises missions and church planting rather than construction of mega churches.[17] In the span of seven years, the church planted over twenty churches all over Kenya, each with several out stations. The membership in all these churches varies from over a few people to over five hundred depending on the location and demographic composition. Pastor Kondia claims that the membership has been growing and is consistent. Though the numbers may not appear significant, the impact of RCCG cannot be underestimated. Their commitment to reaching the unevangelised and thus venturing into the rural areas, sets them apart from other Pentecostal churches, who concentrate only on evangelising the urban areas.

Winners Chapel international

Like the RCCG, Winners Chapel is also concerned with missions. The church was founded by Bishop David Oyedepo in 1981. He was previously a member of Benson Idahosa's Church of God Mission. On 1st May 1981, he experienced what he describes as his commission. During a dream that lasted 18 hours, God said to him 'Now the hour has come to liberate the world from all oppressions of the Devil, through the preaching of the word of faith. And I am sending you to undertake this task.'[18] These oppressions of the devil have been interpreted as poverty, witchcraft and all forms of evil. He views himself as a herald with a message, and says 'no evil can therefore confuse me.' In his own estimation he is not a preacher but a

---

17 Ibid.

18 David Oyedepo, *Wonders of the Age: The Manifestations of Sons of God*, Lagos: Dominion Publishing House, 1996, 7.

'messenger sent to bring heaven on earth.'[19] Together with others, Oyedepo helped to advance the prosperity gospel in Nigeria. He has been influenced by both the American Word of Faith movement and proponents of the gospel of prosperity and their writings.[20]

Winners Chapel was established in Nairobi in 1995. The founding pastors were Bishop Dayo Oluteyo and pastor Olabagun. They were initially hosted by Bishop Arthur Kitonga of the Redeemed Gospel Church. He introduced them to Pentecostal pastors and Christians. Eventually they separated from Bishop Kitonga and established fellowships at the Young Men's Christian Association Hall, Nairobi, and at the University of Nairobi's Taifa Hall. Their message was very well received. The church grew at such a tremendous rate that it was soon accused of using occult powers to attract people to the church, particularly the wealthy. Soon Winners Chapel acquired a plot in a strategic place in Nairobi, Adam's Arcade, where it erected a two thousand seat sanctuary. It is currently building a twenty five thousand seater sanctuary on Mombasa Road, Nairobi.

Victorious Faith Assembly.

Victorious Faith Assembly was founded by Pastor Paul Aigboje, the Bishop elect and leader of Christ Victorious International Churches in Nigeria. The latter was founded in 1992. Pastor Aigboje allegedly experienced a calling in which God gave him a commission based on Jeremiah 1:10. His is a ministry to the nations. His mandate is to 'raise leaders and build up people of God.'[21] The church is headquartered in Abuja, Nigeria. It is quite young but engages in vigorous missionary activity in Nigeria, Asia and Europe. Aigboje was previously a member of the Deeper Life Bible Church in Lagos where he was a pastor. He was disenchanted by the legalism of Deeper Life and its lack of concern for deliverance. His interest in Kenya as a mission frontier arose in a context in which he interprets as prophetic. While at a Christian leaders' conference in Abuja, pastors where asked to stand on the map of Africa and pray for all nations. He stood on Kenya, and he interpreted this as a sign to engage in missionary

---

19 Ibid.

20 Grady 'Nigerian Miracle', 44.

21 Pastor Peter Karanja, Oral Interview, Nairobi 15 February 2003.

activities in Kenya. In 1999, he was invited to a conference in Kisumu, Kenya, entitled 'Unity for Africa'. There he met leaders of Pentecostal/Charismatic churches in Kenya and was subsequently invited to be a speaker in various evangelistic fora within Kenya. Occasionally he was a guest of Pastor Puis Muiru of Maximum Miracle Centre.

He arrived in Nairobi in 2001 and founded Victorious Faith Assembly. The church was housed in a building on Accra Road, but in January 2003 it moved to the basement of Sonalux House, Moi Avenue. It has a membership of about three hundred people so far, though there are many people who have casual unaffiliated relationship with the church. The church has a Bible school which so far has trained thirty two pastors, both men and women. The plan of the church is to train missionaries and enable them to plant churches. There are plans to found new churches around the country even in Uganda. Like Winners Chapel International and RCCG, Victorious Faith Assembly focuses on teaching of the word, deliverance ministry and founding missions.

Teaching and Theology

As charismatic and Pentecostal organisations, the three churches share certain basic teachings that are common to Pentecostals, old and new. They also share common doctrines with the mother churches from which they separated and to which they add their own insights and revelations. The divine revelation and calling through commissions, in which the founders locate their respective churches, feature prominently within them.

The three churches share the following central doctrines: the Bible as God's revelation and unerring eternal message, belief in the trinity, believer's baptism by immersion, baptism of the Holy Spirit, prayer, and confession of sins, divine healing, deliverance, holiness, justification, restitution and sanctification, evangelism and the use of anointing oil for healing. It is however, possible to identify different emphases in the three churches. While Winners Chapel upholds the prosperity gospel and use of different emblems for healing (for example anointing oil, the blood of sprinkling, feet washing and the mantle), the RCCG lays greater emphasis on holiness and evangelism, which is evident in their establishment of missions. Victorious Faith Assembly is basically a teaching church. Their teachings, though not new, are presented with such vigour and vitality that they sound new and appealing. The teachings are often backed up with personal testimonies that make them relevant to their particular situations. As Ojo observes about the teaching of Deeper Life, one can therefore only talk of doctrinal emphasis rather than of new teachings.[22] The major teachings are examined below.

Salvation

For people to call themselves Christians, they must undergo a conversion experience which is described as 'being saved' or being "born again." Salvation is a process which starts by one's realisation of one's sinfulness and the appropriate repentance. On being saved, one is expected to make amends with the past sins or pay recompense where necessary. This is called restitution. Without restitution according to RCCG and Victorious Faith Assembly, one cannot be "born again." After paying restitution, one is considered justified before God and subsequently must pray to be sanctified through receiving the Holy Spirit. Sanctification is viewed as an event and a process. Receiving the Holy Spirit which is viewed as a second baptism (manifested in speaking in tongues), could accompany the moment of conversion or appear later.

Members are therefore urged to pray for and strive to receive the Holy Spirit. Salvation therefore starts with repentance, restitution, justification and sanctification. Sanctification enables one to be Christ like in heart, attitude, disposition, motive and action. Since the sanctification condition can be lost, one must constantly pray and separate oneself from evil. Being "born again" and sanctified empowers the "born again" Christian in his or her battle against sin and temptation. The work of the Holy Spirit in the "born again" Christian is evident in the good moral living, Christian fellowship, and generally in the moral quality of one's life. In order to maintain the sanctified experience, one must also observe some moral regulations. The sanctified must therefore avoid smoking, swearing (cursing, blasphemy), witchcraft, dressing immodestly, and keeping the

---

22 Ojo, "Deeper Life Bible Church of Nigeria,"142.

company of evil doers and those not "born again." Salvation therefore means a positive life of love, fellowship, victory and protection. This process is a preparation for a better future in heaven.

As Magesa observes, most Pentecostal churches espouse an apocalyptic or millennial hope. This therefore, implies that, 'for the chosen "the born again" there is a future time of great prosperity and happiness'.[23] Hence the desire to evangelise and prepare people for heaven in these "last days." While RCCG may be described as pre-millenialist (despite its involvement in social action), the Winners Chapel International, with its prosperity gospel, preaches an immediate "rapture" in its advocacy for attaining wealth and success in the here and now as a sign of God's blessings. Salvation, deliverance and prosperity are therefore viewed as related.

This theology of salvation shows a radical departure from the concept of salvation in mainline Christianity. The perspective of the three churches is similar to the concept of salvation in the East African Revival, which held that salvation is synonymous with a new birth and takes place in a particular moment in the life of a person. From that moment on, one is guaranteed eternal life and is not capable of sinning. To the Catholics, for example, 'salvation is an ongoing process…one is not totally saved until one enters heaven.'[24]

Another feature concerns the Pentecostal churches' individualistic understanding of salvation. The emphasis is not on entering a community of faith but on the personal realisation of the individual of "being saved" and consequently entering into a personal relationship with Jesus. The community of faith becomes a focal point of witnessing to one's salvation. Related to this is also an exclusionist view of salvation. To these churches just like the Pentecostals/ Charismatic, salvation only belongs to those who acknowledge Jesus as their personal saviour. Those who die without accepting Christ are doomed to hell, whether they are non-Christians or "non-born again" Christians in mainline churches. Today Catholics by contrast have accepted the possibility of salvation for individuals who live outside

---

23 Laurenti Magesa, 'Movements and Communities of Affliction,' *Charismatic Revival in Africa* ed. Mika Vahakangas and Andrew A. Kyomo, Nairobi: Acton Publishers, 2003, 28.

24 Aylward Shorter, 'Theology and the New Religious Movements,' *Hekima Review* 26, (December 2001): 14-17.

the 'Christian dispensation, whether before the Christ event or outside the Christian communion after it.'[25]

The Pentecostals see no value in African indigenous religions and also despise mainline Christianity for its formalism and "spirit of religion." They therefore cannot accept that African religion can be a preparation for the Gospel. The focus of their ministry is to deliver and disconnect believers from their cursed or doomed past. There is no gain saying that such an attitude creates a barrier, not only to ecumenism within Christianity, but also with other religions. It is imperative that Pentecostal/Charismatic churches appreciate religious pluralism. They also need to recognise that other Christian denominations are ecclesial communities and channels of God's revelation.

Power of Evil and Deliverance

Scholars have observed that traditional African beliefs of evil and desire for deliverance and power are evident in Pentecostal churches. Kalu rightly states that the major contribution of African Pentecostalism to African Christianity is

> How they address the continued reality of the forces expressed in African cultural forms. Contrary to the early missionary attitude which urged rejection, Pentecostals take the African map of the universe seriously, accepting that culture is both a redemptive gift as well as capable of being hijacked.[26]

Richard Gray too asserts that 'one of the deepest and most enduring desires of all African societies is the anxiety to eliminate evil.'[27]

One of the assumptions of this paper is that Nigerian-founded Pentecostal churches are popular in Kenya because of the way they deal with evil in all its manifestations. Though evil is manifested in witchcraft beliefs and practices and other concepts in the African

---

25 Ibid.

26 Kalu, *Power, Poverty and Prayer: The Challenges of Poverty and Pluralism in African Christianity 1960*, Frankfurt: Peter Long, 2000, 118.

27 Richard Gray, *Black Christians and White Missionaries*, New Haven and London, 1990, 5.

cosmology are persistent and prevalent in Kenya, these beliefs have been vehemently denied in the mainline churches.

The classical African instituted churches, particularly the spiritual ones have recognised and addressed this reality. Their approach has however, been inadequate, since as Kalu observes, it has been limited to destruction and disconnection but not to reconstruction of reality.[28] Pentecostal churches' theology therefore facilitates "believers" to reconstruct their world view. Misty L. Bastian observes that belief in spiritual forces is very prevalent in West Africa. Writing about Nigeria, especially of the Igbo people, she argues that they have close ties to the spirit world. Hence belief in *Mammy Water*, the water goddess of the Igbo, Ibibio and Ijaw peoples of South-western Nigeria, still pervade the perspectives of evil and misfortune in this religion.[29] This spirit is associated with wealth and children and help in times of hardship, illness and need. In Pentecostal/Charismatic rhetoric, veneration of this spirit and others is portrayed in a very negative light and is associated with misfortunes. Consequently, Christian films and literature entering Kenya from Nigeria depict scenes of men and women suffering because they made covenants with water spirits. Whatever benefits may accrue from being bonded to those spirits is considered to be evil. For people to prosper, they have to be disconnected through prayer and exorcism from such spirits and attendant covenants. Beliefs about magic and witchcraft therefore feature prominently in videos and films. These images have fired the imaginations of Kenyans. Not only has the literature, reawakened and reinforced their realisation of the pervasiveness of evil, but it has helped them to see that Pentecostal Christianity has the power to enable them to overcome this evil. It gives them the spiritual resources to do so.

---

28 Kalu, *Power, Poverty and Prayer*, 118.

29 *Mammy Water* are female water spirits that are believed to reincarnate in human forms and visit untold suffering on human beings particularly men. This is a belief found among the Ibibio, Ijaw and Igbo speaking people of South-eastern Nigeria. *Ogbaanje* are spirits which manifest themselves to be born into the world of human beings. Misty L. Bastian, "Married in the Water: Spirit Kin and other afflictions of Modernity in South Eastern Nigeria," *Journal of Religion in Africa* 27, no. 2, 1997, 117. See also Francis A. Arinze, *Sacrifice in Igbo Religion*, Ibadan: Ibadan University Press, 1970, 14 and 15.

Pentecostals perceive the visible world as a mirror of the spiritual one, hence material, evil, social and political processes are also affected by evil happenings in the spiritual realm. This holistic view of reality is present both in African Traditional and Hebrew world views. It seems that the Pentecostals have synthesised traditional beliefs about evil and those in the Bible. Hence Kalu argues that

> African Pentecostals have equated principalities, powers and demons with various categories in their world view and as enemies of God and man. They reinforce the causality pattern in the primal world view before providing a solution beyond the purviews of indigenous cosmology.[30]

This synthesis in beliefs in witchcraft and demonology has been described as "witch demonology" by Opuku Onyina.[31] Kenyan Pentecostals, like their Nigerian counterparts, have been influenced by the writings of Derek Prince and others on the subject of deliverance. Prince sees the connection between the occult and demonology and argues, 'as we trace the deceptive paths of demonic activity and the occult, we discover that they all proceed from one primal source, witchcraft.'[32]

In view of this pervasiveness of evil, Pentecostals have evolved a powerful deliverance ministry that addresses the issues and problems that deny people's well being, prosperity, success, and abundant life. The churches train people to avoid any immoral activity that would expose them to demonic possession. Deliverance extends not only to individuals, "born again" or not, but to nations as well.[33] This

---

30 Kalu, *Power, Poverty and Prayer*, 119.

31 Opoku Oyinah, "*Contemporary 'Witchdemonology' in Africa*," unpublished paper, 2002, 4.

32 Derek Prince, *They Shall Expel Demons: What You Need to Know about Demons: Your Invisible Enemies*, Harpenden: Derek Prince Ministries, 1998, 141.

33 It is believed that being "born again" is not enough, for one may still be subject to ancestral and generational curses. This could affect one's wellbeing and prosperity. Belief in territorial spirits is also perceived by some to be responsible for Africa's problems. It is also assumed that all evil acts have their demonic counterparts. See Peter C. Wagner ed. *Engaging the Enemy: How to fight and Defend Territorial Spirits*, Ventura: Regal, 1993; Emeka Nwankpa, *Redeeming the Land; Interceding for the Nation*, Achimota, Ghana: Christian Africa Press, 1994, 9; and Chris O. Oshun "Spirits and Healing in a Depressed Economy: The Case of Nigeria, *Mission Studies* 25, no. 1 1998:33.

deliverance ministry, as Opoku observes, blends Western Christian concepts of demonology and exorcism and African traditional beliefs and practices.

The three churches in this study offer a deliverance ministry. Winner's chapel International mediates deliverance through "teaching of the word of God". The word of God is depicted as having power. It is lack of its knowledge that leads people to destruction. Oyedepo writes,

> God's word makes you smarter than the devil. The word of God carries the divine nature of God which is transferred to you when it is formed in you and becomes your lifestyle. A simple command from you based on the authority and integrity of the word of God which when mixed with faith in you, will release the trigger of heaven's wisdom.[34]

Eileen Njeri, an evangelist in Winners Chapel, confirms that the teaching on the word is a unique contribution of this church to Kenyan Christianity.[35] Members are taught to "take authority" in all situations "standing on the word." It is this power, when uttered, that is "supernatural" and "potent" and that "destroys" and disconnects believers and victims from witchcraft and evil machinations visible and invisible. This "word" also empowers believers to live righteous lives, to acquire new identities, to reorient their lives, to be affirmed and face life confidently. It also enables them to seal all loopholes that can render them vulnerable to demonic possession. The Bible is envisioned as containing resources necessary for their reconstruction of a new reality of well being.

The reconstructed world is sustained by individuals and the church community through continuous messages of affirmation depicted on billboards, bumper stickers and banners in the church. Kalu calls this 'bumper stickers hermeneutics.'[36] Hence, in Winners Chapel, affirmation messages such as "it is my time to shine," "my hour of grace will come," and "it is my time to prosper" abound. This "bumper sticker" theology is most pervasive in Nigerian-founded

---

34 Oyedepo, *Wonders of the Age*, 10.

35 Eileen Njeri, Oral Interview, Nairobi, 10 March, 2003

36 Kalu, *Power, Poverty and Prayer*, 125.

churches; although it is also evident in other Kenyan charismatic churches such as Maximum Miracle Centre and Jesus is Alive Ministries. The "word" therefore is depicted as powerful, and it plays a major role in spiritual formation. Pastor Pamela Ogwel of Victorious Faith Assembly describes it as 'food for the spirit.'[37] Without it, a believer cannot withstand the wiles of the enemy. It helps one to resist forces that can lead to backsliding. In the Pentecostal churches, members carry notebooks and pens to write down the "word" from the "servant of God" that will nourish them spiritually and give them power to overcome evil. Along with the word, anointing oil is used in the three churches. Oyedepo defines it as

> The spirit of God mysteriously put in the bottle which is mysteriously designed to communicate the power of God bodily. It is the power of God in your hand, in the person of the Holy Spirit, to humiliate Satan. It is God's standard against every invasion of the enemy. The anointing oil is able to end all frustrations in your life. When it touches the barren woman, she becomes abundantly fruitful. When it touches anyone chained by the devil, the person becomes automatically free. There is no sickness or disease of any kind that can escape the power of anointed oil.[38]

The anointing oil idea is derived from the Bible. In the Old Testament, it was used for sanctification, healing, and appointments of priests and kings.[39] Derek Prince acknowledges this usage and regards it as an emblem, a vehicle to transmit blessing. It works only if there is faith and obedience. He also precludes any magical interpretations in its use.[40]

In the Winners Chapel, however, application of anointing oil in healing, deliverance, and protection has acquired magical connotations. Some people drink, bathe, cook food, and anoint surfaces and objects

---

37 Pamela Ogwel, Oral Interview, Nairobi 14 February, 2003.

38 Oyedepo, *Wonders of the Age*, 25-26.

39 See Exodus 30:22-33; Leviticus 8:1-12; 1 Samuel 16:13; 1 Cor. 10:16; James 5: 13-18; Hebrews 12:22-24.

40 Derek Prince, *Blessing or Curse: You Can Choose*, Grand Rapids, Michigan: Chosen Books, 1990, 34-35.

with it. This has raised objections against the church by other Pentecostals. Despite some negative appellatives, anointing oil is viewed as "a weapon of the spirit" by most Pentecostal churches. The RCCG and Victorious Faith Assembly use it in a restricted way, mainly during miracle services and prayers for healing. Other acts and objects viewed as "weapons of the spirit" by Winners Chapel are the "mantle," "feet washing," the "blood of sprinkling," and "the communion." The mantle is a "sanctified" item of clothing belonging to a sick or suffering person, or a "born again" Christian. It is used as a sacramental, and is too believed to mediate healing. Usually handkerchiefs are used as mantles. Testimonies abound of how anointing oil and mantles provided members with protection and salvation from evil and difficult circumstances. This theology of deliverance is thus a prominent feature in the three churches.

Mission and Evangelism
Evangelism is a major focus of Nigerian Pentecostalism in Kenya. The three churches regard it as their most important work. RCCG sees the object of its mission as 'to make heaven, to take as many people as possible with us;...to plant churches within five minutes walking distance in every city and town of developing countries and within five minutes driving distance of developed countries.'[41] The goal of evangelism is to take the cross across frontiers primarily for conversion. The mission initiative is cross cultural and is directed not mainly to the non-Christians but to Christians in other denominations. The purpose is to create awareness of salvation by exposing people to gospel values and realities. However, the conventional meaning of mission as an outward bound, cross-cultural and cross-religious drive is not totally absent. Kenyans in these churches have made endeavours to "convert" Hindus, Muslims, and adherents of traditional African religion or those who have not yet been reached by the gospel. Thus RCCG have made efforts to penetrate communities in rural areas. As Mathew Ojo observes about charismatics in Nigeria, 'evangelism is seen as a work of redemption to loosen and free human beings from the grips of evil spirits, witches, forces of darkness, principalities,

---

41 Redeemed Christian Church of God, *Solution Bulletin* RCCG, (23 March 2003), 2.

enemies, bad luck and repeated failures, all of which are prevalent in the African world view.'[42]

The response to culturally perceived illnesses and problems may be one of the major factors of the appeal of healing and deliverance ministries of these churches. Eileen Njeri is emphatic that Nigerian charismatic churches and pastors have enabled their members to understand 'the hidden things of the enemy. They have taught us secrets to destroy the works of the devil and to flee from him.'[43]

They have also helped them to see the relationship between evangelism and societal transformation. They have come to realize that problems in the social, political and economic realms are due to the sins of individuals and society. The churches see themselves 'ideally as providing moral and spiritual guidance, hope and personal empowerment,'[44]as well as building spiritual communities. It is such individuals and communities that can bring about social and political reform when they are united in a serving relationship with Christ. Evangelism is viewed by the Pentecostals as providing an alternative approach to address the problems bedeviling Africa, hence the "word" must be preached to all in order to bring about the required transformation. This author agrees with Ojo that 'evangelism has indeed provided charismatics with an alternative for coming to terms with contemporary conditions.'[45] The three churches utilize a variety of methods for evangelism which include door to door evangelism and a variety of literature including handbills, crusades, bible study, and personal evangelism, a variety of daily services, monthly conferences and home cell fellowships. Members and participants are inspired to witness to Christ and are motivated to exploit their human faculties, encounters and opportunities to share their faith with others both in private and in public.

Linked to evangelism is the concept of the development of the whole person in relationship to the environment. Pastor Ogwel of Victorious Faith Assembly perceives this concept as what attracted her

---

42 Ojo, *"The Charismatic Movement in Nigeria Today,"* 116.

43 Eileen Njeri, Oral Interview, Nairobi, 10 March, 2003.

44 Marshall, *"God is not a Democrat,"* 241.

45 Ojo, "The Charismatic Movement in Nigeria Today," 116.

to the church. Although the three churches have not been deeply involved in social activism, the idea is not absent. They all started by establishing bible schools to train missionaries for evangelism. They plan to offer social services such as education and health care. However, they encourage every member to be involved in "kingdom service," interpreted as participation in at least one church activity. The churches have built a concerned and caring community which particularly offers women and youth renewal and hope. This category of people has not found fulfilment in mainline Christianity. The roles of women vary in the three churches. While RCCG and Victorious Church Assembly ordain women as pastors, Winners Chapel ordains them as "daughters of the church." This has therefore led to women who feel themselves called to the ordained ministry to leave Winners Chapel. All the same, the teachings about respect for just authority within home, church and society are tenets of Nigeria Pentecostal churches that are admired.

Nigerian Pentecostal churches have not involved themselves in political processes in Kenya and are not members of any Pentecostal ecumenical association such as the United Evangelical Churches of Kenya. They have, however, indirectly influenced politics though their teaching on spiritual forces behind political events. They have therefore facilitated the development of the intercessory ministry through which Christians can be involved in the prophetic and prayer ministry of interceding for the nation and its rulers. All these activities are viewed as evangelism.

Discussion and Conclusion
This chapter has so far reviewed the Nigerian Pentecostal Missionary Enterprise in Kenya through three Pentecostal or charismatic churches. The question however, still lingers; why do Nigerian missionaries go to Kenya? What impact has this missionary enterprise had on Kenyans? What theologies and practices of mission do they bring? Rosalind Hackett has noted the resurgence of religious activities in Nigeria in the past three decades and attributes it to the phenomenal growth and popularity of Christian charismatic and Pentecostal movements. She sees this resurgence as part of the globalizing cultural forces, creativity, and innovation of Nigerians as

well as of their natural mobility, whether for trade or other endeavours.[46]

Nigerians have always had trade and diplomatic relations with Kenya. Some Kenyans have wondered whether the revival from Nigeria is genuine or a cover for trading and possibly sinister activities. In fact, Winners Chapel, despite its wide appeal has been viewed by some as a cult propagating strange doctrines. It is said to be elitist and anti-social. The emphases on holy living, time management and avoidance of time wasting social activities have been interpreted by some as signs of cultic elements. Tensions between Nigerian and Kenyan churches are also exacerbated by Nigerian proselytizing techniques. They are seen to be aggressive, not only because of their use of multi media, but also in their encroachment into some areas where Kenyan Pentecostal churches have not reached. Where as RCCG and Winners Chapel have managed to go to both major urban and rural towns in Kenya, most of the larger and newer Pentecostal churches still limit their ministries to Nairobi and its environs. Hence it is not surprising that the Nigerian churches have been accused of "sheep stealing" and manipulating their adherents through their "seed faith" doctrine. A sizeable number of families are impoverished through putting their resources to the service of the church. Anticipated "financial miracles" rarely occur.[47] Although this doctrine is common to all churches that subscribe to the gospel of prosperity, the fact that "foreigners" are seen to advocate the doctrine more aggressively than the locals makes their motives circumspect. Some Nigerians have been accused by the media of peddling drugs. This has led to the popular suspicion that Nigerian churches are covert operations for laundering drug money.[48]

Nevertheless, those who have been in the churches for a long time attribute their appeal to their doctrine on the "word of faith," concern for missions, and upholding of gospel values. Their commitment to

46 Rosalind Hackett, 'Radical Christian Revivalism in Nigeria and Ghana: Recent Patterns of Intolerance and Conflict,' in *Religion and Human Rights: Proselization and Community Self-Determination in Africa,* ed. Abdullahi Ahmed An-Na' im, New York: Maryknoll, Orbis Books, 1999, 248.

47 Abijah Nyaga, Oral Interview, Nairobi, March 2003.

48 Fred Omwoyo, Oral Interview, March, 2003. cf. Frank Brown, 'Taking Kiev by Surprise' *Charisma*, 28, no. 11, June 2003, 89-92.

evangelism is such that they provide subsidized transport to Sunday services to people living outside the city. It is the strangeness of these practices that elicit suspicion. Kenyans are not aware that free transport and subsidized spiritual retreats have been practiced in Nigeria for a long time, for example, in the Deeper Life Bible Church.

The Nigerian Pentecostals have helped their Kenyan clientele to have a deeper understanding of the healing and deliverance ministry. Due to their social contexts where the power of evil is not denied but confronted, they have availed Kenyans with spiritual and social resources to overcome evil. Application of healing is quite extensive, covering every possible area of life: personal aspirations, national issues, employment, health, family life, education and faith. Through their mediation of healing in a communal context, these churches provide social and even material support to members who need solutions to their experiences of uncertainty and other forces threatening their lives in the drastically changed social, economic, political, and religious moral order. In their approach to evangelism, they have attempted to be sensitive to the local cultures and not to impose their cultural idiosyncrasies. However it is also evident that aspects of Nigerian concepts of evil, for example the *Mummy Water* spirits and others have been incorporated into the Kenyan repertoire of evil. Focus on exorcism and deliverance has probably resuscitated and reinforced belief in the pervasiveness of evil.

The Nigerian Pentecostals have attempted to reshape the lives of their members along biblical lines. In so doing, they have been overzealous in repudiating traditional and cultural practice. Adoption of this theology has been perceived as destructive to family life when Christians are encouraged to break ties with the unsaved.[49] They also have ambivalent attitudes towards women who though are given greater avenues in leadership and participation in church life may also be stigmatized due to the strict moral stance of the churches and their traditional, stereotypical perception as the cause of men's moral weakness etc. This is a view that pervades most of the video and audio cassettes and is an area of further tension. Women are depicted as behind the collapse of many churches, homes and men's moral standing. The video cassettes are also regarded as a strategy to market

49 Abijah Nyaga, Oral Interview, Nairobi, March 2003.

the churches. Through capitalizing on people's fear of witchcraft, Ukah observes, the church develops a desire among members to consult the Pentecostal pastor and the 'consumption of deliverance services, prayer meetings and other paraphernalia.'[50] This is a proselytizing strategy which, judging from the way some Kenyans consume those videos and literature has had an impact on marketing the Nigerian brand of Pentecostalism. Some Christians regard the theology portrayed in the videos as enslaving and that it masks the love of God. The great appeal of deliverance and intercession conferences and miracle anointing services is, however, evidence of the need for this ministry as provided in the churches.

Nigerian Pentecostal churches have had a positive impact on Kenyan Christianity, particularly in Nairobi where people have access to the various aspects of these ministries. They have encouraged professionals such as lawyers to offer free services to poor members of the church. They have succeeded in impressing upon all members of their importance in the church as individuals as well as through the services they render. They have created space for empowerment for members and transformed the lives of many who have been lost to drugs, alcohol, hopelessness and despair. Teachings on business, positive thinking and self esteem have also contributed in the development of provision of a holistic ministry. The gospel of prosperity has even enabled members to have aspirations and to believe in themselves. Affirmation and self confidence built on tenets of faith are the first steps to an individual's transformation

The Nigerian Pentecostal missionary enterprise in Kenya has built on previous revival experiences in Kenya since the 1920's. Though the numbers of Kenyan members may not be very large compared to other local Pentecostal churches, their impact in terms of spiritual transformation of individuals' lives cannot be underestimated. Given their express desire to found new missions all over Kenya, Eastern, Central and Southern Africa, their impact will no doubt be pervasive.

This chapter has underscored the need for the study of the significance of intra-African mission endeavours which has been

---

50 Asonzeh F. K Ukah, "Advertising God: Nigerian Christian Video Films and the Power of Consumer Culture," *Journal of Religion in Africa* 33, no.2 2003, 227.

ignored due to too much focus on Diasporaic Christianity. This dimension of mission is related to migration in terms of the cross cultural nature of Christian mission. Though not directly related to African migrant Christianity in Europe or within Africa, it is significant for the purpose of the continued renewal of the church in Africa and the rest of the world though Africa.

Chapter Four

Mission perspectives among Pentecostal West Indian religious communities in New York City and London: 'By My Spirit' says the Lord [1]

Janice McLean

The present status of global Christianity has been greatly influenced by two developments. First there has been the notable shift of the centre of Christianity from the North to the South. This suggests that the beliefs and practices expressed within the southern continents may have a greater influence on the Christianity typical of the Twenty-first century.[2] Second, the existence of several global and local socio-economic and political forces are uniting to shape the world into one global village, in which nation state boundaries are becoming more permeable allowing for greater movement of goods, ideas and people from one nation state to another.[3] This permeability as well as the shift in the centre of Christianity has resulted in the emergence of a new

---

1   The role of the Holy Spirit in the lives of Pentecostal believers is paramount. It is the Holy Spirit who is believed to be the one who enables and equips an individual for ministry. As such the Pentecostal believers are encouraged to be filled with and led by the Spirit in all that they endeavour to do. Several biblical texts that are used to support this dependence upon the Holy Spirit are: Acts 1:8; Zechariah 4:6b. See also Robert Mapes Anderson, *Vision of the Disinherited: The making of American Pentecostalism* (New York: Oxford University Press, 1979) p. 41; Robert Beckford, *Dread and Pentecostal: A Political Theology for the Black Church in Britain* (London: Society for Promoting Christian Knowledge, 2000) p. 6.

2   Andrew F. Walls, *The Cross-Cultural Process in Christian History* (New York: Orbis Books, 2002), p. 85. Alister E. McGrath *The Future of Christianity* (Oxford: Blackwell Publishers Ltd, 2002); Philip Jenkins *The Next Christendon: The coming of Global Christianity* (New York: Oxford University Press, 2002); Viggo Mortensen, 'What is happening to global Christianity?' *Dialog* 43 (1) 2004, pp. 20-27.

3   Doris M. Meissner, Robert D. Hormats, Antonio Garigues Walker, Shijuro Ogata, *International Migration Challenges in a New Era.* (New York: The Trilateral Commission, 1993) p. 89.

expression of Christianity – Southern Christianity as lived out in the North. This Southern Christianity, not only brings with it a vibrant and expressive worship style but also several dynamic missionary perspectives, focused on the re-evangelization of the West.[4]

Within the diaspora context, West Indian Christians are faced with various socio-economic and political factors that have served to shape their lives and religious practices in profound ways. It will be imperative to ascertain not only what these factors are but more importantly how their lives and religious practices have been shaped within these diaspora contexts. What missionary perspectives do the West Indian migrants bring with them upon migration? How are these perspectives articulated and/or re-formulated within that specific context? How does the existence of different host contexts influence this process? How are these mission perspectives shaped within an intergenerational context? How do these missionary perspectives relate to the negotiation of identities, boundaries and margins that occur within these religious communities? In this chapter, by examining the data generated from a comparative study based on interviews and ethnographic fieldwork of Pentecostal West Indian religious communities in New York City and London[5], I will seek to highlight some of the complexities involved in addressing the questions documented above with the express aim of investigating how mission is being conceptualized and practiced within these immigrant communities

Throughout this chapter the term West Indian will be used in a collective sense to denote the people from the Caribbean islands that were once a part of the British Empire. Despite this designation, it is imperative to note that this term also incorporates a diversity of identities, and cultures. For although each island shares a common British heritage, they still have their own distinctive cultures and identities. It is also important to note that the term West Indian is a

---

4   Historically the West was perceived by the Christians in the Southern hemisphere as the bulwark of Christianity. This perception has proved to be a fallacy as they have encountered an increasingly secularized and pluralistic society.

5   Ethnographic fieldwork and interviews were conducted within three Pentecostal West Indian immigrant religious communities. Flatlands Church of God and Miracle Temple Ministries Inc. in New York City and Willesden New Testament Church of God in London.

product of the diaspora[6]. For as the migrants interacted with their 'host countries' some of their individual cultures expressions and distinctive identities became less pronounced and more collective ones emerged. This was especially the case in the social and political contexts.

The Missionary Perspectives within Pentecostal West Indian Immigrant churches

The missionary perspectives that became evident within Pentecostal West Indian religious communities in the diaspora are essentially the by-product of the convergence of two elements: the immigrants' faith – which also included mission perspectives; and their interaction with their environment.

West Indian Christianity

The Christianity and the resulting mission perspectives that the immigrants brought with them to their new social contexts was a complex synthesis of an African religious heritage, eighteenth-century missionary[7] movements and twentieth-century Pentecostal mission activities. Each of these three belief systems, which are within themselves diverse, provided the messages, interpretations and practices that became instrumental in the religious lives of the immigrants. Thus the gospel preached by the missionaries, was decoded and understood by the slaves through the interpretive framework of their African religious heritage. It was this message that was later articulated in various practices noted within Pentecostalism[8]. The result of this process was multifaceted, producing a faith that comprised of both the compensatory and prophetic mindsets and upheld the primacy of evangelism as a mission perspective[9]. The

---

6   Within the region the national identities take precedence and as such this collective term is rarely used.

7   These missionaries were associated with the Moravian, Methodist and Baptist denominations.

8   Within the Pentecostal tradition, great emphasis is placed on the imminent return of Christ. As a consequence, evangelism of the 'lost' takes centre stage in many of the many programmes and aspects of the church.

9   See the Church of God website: http://www.churchofgod.cc/about/church_is.cfm, section entitled Evangelistic and World Mission and see also the commendation given to the New Testament Church of God in Jamaica by their parent body – Church of God for

compensatory or 'otherworldly' mindset focuses on surviving and spiritually overcoming the evil influences of the world, in order to go home to heaven, where the individual will be rewarded. By contrast, the prophetic or 'this-worldy' mindset translates "the Christian teaching of the worth of every human being [...] into a culture of protest"[10]; whereby there is active engagement with individuals and systems in order to transform the society.[11] For the majority of West Indian Christians, it was the compensatory mindset that remained dominant within their lives[12]. Thus, the gospel propagated in the forms of personal evangelism, distributing biblical leaflets, and open air meetings, was mainly about personal salvation. It did not openly advocate active engagement with the community or the socio-economic political forces within the society. On the periodic occasions when attention was paid to secular activities, they were concentrated in the area of welfare.[13] Another characteristic of this mission perspective is the focus on local evangelism. Very little attention was given towards developing and engaging in evangelism on a regional or global scale[14].

---

their "undaunted courage and determination to evangelize the land of Jamaica", see website: http://www.ntcgjaci.org/history.htm.

10 Shirley C. Gordon, *God Almighty Make Me Free: Christianity in Pre-emancipation Jamaica* (Bloomington: Indiana University Press, 1996) pp.138

11 Evidence is visible in the case of Jamaica in both the Baptist war of 1831 and the Morant Bay Rebellion of 1865.

12 As the Christians prepared themselves for heaven, they were admonished to work hard and live a good life. They were also taught to obey the religious and secular authorities. As a result this mindset helped to perpetuate a system oriented towards Britain. Exceptions to this were: the independent indigenous congregation within the Baptist denomination that had some prophetic tendencies; Bedwardism and Garveyism.

13 These include visiting the sick, aiding others during natural disasters, and other forms of benevolence ministries.

14 In both the Baptist and Church of Scotland denominations various efforts were made to engage in missionary ventures to Africa by Christians in the West Indies. Their efforts were deemed by their superiors to be overzealous and premature, not reflecting the state on dependency that these denominations within the West Indies were in. Although some teams were sent out, this missionary thrust was not sustained or reproduced in those that followed them.

The diaspora reality: Encountering the Motherland and the Promise land[15]

Historically, the West Indies have maintained a strong regional and international migratory culture. So for many who travelled to Britain and the United States, they were following in the footsteps of those who had left their island home for other lands. Like their predecessors, this journey that they embarked upon was not conducted in a haphazard manner but was fuelled by various images that the immigrants sought to verify i.e. Britain as the motherland and the United States as the promise land.

United States

The majority of the West Indians who currently reside in the United States came as a result of the Hart-Cellar Immigration Act of 1965. It is imperative to note that upon their arrival, these West Indians did not perceive America through rose tinted windows of racial equality. [16] They came with knowledge of the racial dynamics that operated within the American society. However, upon arrival many West Indians realized that this fore knowledge did not adequately portray their present social contexts. Within the predominantly black communities in which they lived,[17] they encountered an America in which the prejudices attached to members of other races still exist albeit not in as visible a form as it was prior to the Civil Rights Movement. The permanence of this system is reiterated by Derrick Bell who states, 'the racism that made slavery feasible is far from dead in the last decade of

---

15 For the West Indian immigrant to Britain the term motherland signified a sense of belonging. England was perceived as the beneficent mother whose arms would be open to welcome her 'children' as full-fledged members of the family. See: Malcolm Cross, and Han Entzinger, eds., *Lost Illusions: Caribbean Minorities in Britain and the Netherlands* (London: Routlege, 1988) p. 42. Nancy Foner, *Jamaica Farewell: Jamaican Migrants in London* (London: Routledge & Kegan Paul, 1979) p. 41. In contrast the United States in its portrayal as the promise land signified the assurance of a better life and with it opportunities to improve themselves and their families.

16 See Nancy Foner, 'Race and Color: Jamaican Migrants in London and New York City', *International Migration Review*, Vol. 19, No. 4 (Winter 1985) p. 714 – 715.

17 Kyle D. Crowder, 'Residential Segregation of West Indians in the New York/New Jersey Metropolitan Area: The Roles of Race and Ethnicity'. *International Migration Review*, Vol. 33 No. 1 (Spring 1999), p 79.

the twentieth-century America'.[18]   Blatant discrimination had been replaced by a more subtle system, one that married negative stereotypes with various policies that served to relegate Black America to the bottom of the American socio economic and political ladder.[19] Faced with this context, the West Indian immigrants sought to set themselves apart, by 'maintain[ing] the distinction between themselves and American blacks and to avoid relegation to poor black neighbourhoods or to American's most oppressed racial group'.[20] This was accomplished by establishing distinctive residential enclaves, which enabled the immigrants to intentionally preserve their ethnic and cultural heritage.   The enclaves also facilitated the creation of spaces where the immigrants were empowered.   Through the formation of social organizations, especially religious organizations, the immigrants found places where they could occupy various leadership positions, and discover 'ties to job opportunities and interlacing ties which reinforce parental authority and values vis-à-vis the second generation'.[21]

Britain

For the West Indian migrants who came to Britain beginning in 1948, they came with their 'Britishness' relatively intact. They were citizens of the empire, speaking British English, having British manners, knowing British history, and as such they 'belonged'[22]. For many of these immigrants, these cultural and historical markers constituted an essential part of their identity, because within the West

18 Derrick Bell, *Faces at the Bottom of the Well: The Permanence of Racism* (New York: Basic Books, 1992) p. 3.

19 See discussion in Cornell West, *Race Matters*. (Boston: Beacon Press, 1993) and Derrick Bell, *Faces at the Bottom of the Well: The Permanence of Racism* (New York: Basic Books, 1992).

20 Kyle D. Crowder, 'Residential Segregation of West Indians in the New York/New Jersey Metropolitan Area: The Roles of Race and Ethnicity'. *International Migration Review*, Vol. 33 No. 1 (Spring 1999)p.108.

21 Mary C. Waters, 'Ethnic and Racial Identities of Second-Generation Black Immigrants in New York City'. *International Migration Review*, Vol. 28, No.4, Special Issue: The New Second Generation (Winter, 1994) p 804.

22 Foner Nancy, *Jamaica Farewell: Jamaican Migrants in London* (London: Routledge & Kegan Paul, 1979) p. 41.See also: Anita Jackson, *Catching Both Sides of the Wind: Conversations with Five Black Pastors* (London: The British Council of Churches, 1985) p. 88.

Indian context, these elements were internalized and given meaning. This internalization sequentially supplied the immigrants with a medium through which they could articulate who they were, i.e. British citizens, members of the commonwealth, in regards to the 'other' – the rest of the world. However upon arrival, instead of being welcomed as British citizens they were treated with disdain, and a marked coldness. According to Mike Phillips and Trevor Phillips, what the West Indian immigrants encountered was 'an exclusive and impenetrable image of British society, backed up by the ideology of race and racial superiority, which had for so long been an essential pillar of imperial power.'[23] It was an image that declared them 'not welcome'. Their status as British citizens was inconsequential because to the British masses, citizenship, education or proper speech did not make a person British. To be British was to be white and therefore no space was given for their articulation of 'British' identity. Consequently, the immigrants found themselves thrust into 'a moral environment which steadfastly refused to acknowledge change, or the possibility of change, in the nation's self image.'[24] Within this environment they were classified as invaders who had come to corrupt the romanticised pristine British nation[25]. This classification was perpetuated in several areas of society, namely employment, and family life. The West Indian migrant's reactions were diverse. They included: disillusionment, the creation of enclaves and social organizations and active engagement with the society[26]. One organization formed by the immigrants was the Black-led church. Prior to coming to Britain, many immigrants were Anglicans and Methodist. Upon their arrival, many sought out these churches to participate in worship. However, instead of being welcomed, many were met with discrimination and

---

23 Mike Phillips and Trevor Phillips, *Windrush: The irresistible rise of Multi-Racial Britain* (London: HarperCollins Publishers, 1998) p. 4.

24 Ibid., p. 4.

25 The notion of a pristine British nation was a fallacy perpetuated by Enoch Powell and others for political reasons. See: Mike Phillips and Trevor Phillips, *Windrush: The irresistible rise of Multi-Racial Britain* (London: HarperCollins Publishers, 1998).

26 All of these reactions were a way for the immigrants to regain some sort of equilibrium. In each of the reactions the West Indian migrant underwent a process of re-articulation of identity. One in which the interaction with the current social context gave rise to several 'West Indian' identities being celebrated and maintained as well as giving room for the emergence of new ones.

rejection. As a result, many began to attend the Pentecostal Black-led churches that were being formed.[27]

Mission Perspectives

Historically, Pentecostalism has been noted for its narrativity,[28] in that beliefs are normally communicated orally and practised, rather than documented. However in contemporary times, this character has been undergoing marked change due to the growing presence of literature and the use of media and other technology within the practice and articulation of belief. Therefore as we examine the missionary perspectives within Pentecostal West Indian religious communities in New York and London, it will be essential to investigate both what is documented and what is articulated in the pulpits[29] and what is lived out in the lives of the members.

For the three religious communities included in my research, their principal mission is the 'winning of souls' i.e. a religious conversion, in which an individual changes from another belief system to that of Christianity [30]. This mission is kept at the forefront of these ministries

---

27 See Anita Jackson, *Catching Both Sides of the Winds: Conversations with Five Black Pastors* (London: The British Council of Churches, 1985); Paul Grant and Raj, Patel eds., *A Time to Speak: Perspectives of Black Christians in Britain*, (Nottingham: Russell Press, 1990). See also Clifford Hill, *Black Churches: West Indian and African Sects in Britain*, (London: Community and Race relations unit of the British Council of Churches, 1971) who argues that the formation of Black-led church was due to various cultural, social and theological differences between Black people and what existed within White Christianity.

28 Walter J. Hollenweger, "After Twenty Years' Research on Pentecostalism," *International Review of Mission 75* Ja (1986) and Iain MacRobert, *The Black Roots and White Racism of Early Pentecostalism in the USA* (Basingstoke: Macmillan, 1988).

29 Although sermons has long been considered as oral communication with the increased use within Pentecostal religious communities of recording devises, various media technologies and the compiling of sermons for publication, they too have become part of the corpus of written documents, giving expression to the beliefs and practices of these religious communities.

30 See the following websites for Miracle Temple Ministries Inc. http://www.miracle-temple-ministries.org/43/index.html; Willesden New Testament Church of God: http://www.wntcg.org.uk/index.htm. Statements alluding to this focus of the church's ministry are also found within the Sunday bulletin for Flatlands Church of God. Note that this process of conversion involves making certain declarations as noted on Willesden New Testament Church of God website under the section entitled Declaration of Faith, 'that all have sinned and come short of the glory of God and that repentance is

in various forms: it is documented in the church's bulletin, in the visitor's welcome booklets, and on the church's websites; it is declared from the pulpit on a regular basis; and embodied in the altar call which concludes the Sunday Morning Service. According to one informant, 'I love when they do an altar call. If they don't do an altar call on a Sunday Morning I don't feel happy, I go home and feel that coming to church was a waste of time. But if they have altar call and one soul come, I feel more happy than anything, so winning souls is the most important thing.'[31] For all three religious communities the scriptural basis for this mission is the great commission: 'Go therefore and make disciples of all nations, baptising them in the name of the Father and of the Son and of the Holy Spirit, teaching them to observe all things that I have commanded you: and lo, I am with you always even to the end of the age' (Matthew 28:19-20, NKJV). How are these mission perspectives expressed in the diaspora context?

Within both contexts, some mission perspectives are articulated in forms that are similar with the 'home' context. This tendency is however more pronounced within the New York context because of the drive among West Indian migrants to distinguish themselves from black America; the constant influx of new immigrants from the West Indies; and the strength of trans-national ties. Within both contexts, the continuance with 'home' is primarily expressed in the dominance of the personal evangelism within the lives of the church members. Personal evangelism is not limited to a specific space, time or context within their lives – instead it supersedes these boundaries and thus is engaged in on the job, on public transportation, and even on visits to the beauty salon or supermarket. Linked with personal evangelism is the distribution of biblical leaflets called tracts. Within New York context, personal evangelism, in terms of street and public transportation evangelism, is very visible and is sometimes viewed as one of the characteristics of a serious Christian. In Flatlands New Testament Church of God, the chairperson of the evangelism committee periodically submits a report documenting the number of people led to accept Jesus as their personal saviour or 'saved' and the

---

commanded of God for all and necessary for forgiveness of sins. [And] [t]hat justification, regeneration, and the new birth are wrought by faith in the blood of Jesus Christ'.

31 Interview with a 1.5 generation male member of Miracle Temple Ministries Inc.

number of tracts distributed over a certain period of time. This report is incorporated into the church's comprehensive report that is submitted to the denominational headquarters in Tennessee. Note however, that given the residential patterns adapted by the West Indian immigrants in New York City this personal evangelism especially in its public forms – namely evangelism conducted on the street and on public transportation is primarily focused on other West Indian immigrants or ethnic minorities. In London in comparison, the personal evangelism conducted although targeted specifically towards members of the black minority has historically been less visible in terms of a public forum and is more relationship based. This was primarily due to two reasons: the discrimination that immigrants had experienced in their encounter with the members of the White British community; and the anti-social laws within British society which made such public evangelistic forums illegal. For one informant in London, her contact with Willesden New Testament Church of God and her subsequent 'salvation' was a result of a relationship that she developed on the job with a member of the church. The informant states, 'she said come, come to my church, come on and visit my church, come in. It took about four years for me to yield[ing] and then you know the struggle in [the] my workplace was getting intensive so one day I say well I will go with you. But all the time she comes and ask prayer for me, so one day I said I'll go with you. I came.'[32] One dynamic in regards to personal evangelization in particular and evangelism in general that needs to be highlighted in relation to both contexts is the issue of gender implications. Within the congregations it is the objective of the men's ministry to evangelize men and that of the women's ministry to evangelize women[33]. Although there may be exceptions like the ministry teams that conduct home visitations and which comprise of both genders, on the whole this gender designation is encouraged.

---

32 Interview with a first generation African female member of Willesden New Testament Church of God in London.

33 See mission and objectives documented for each ministry within the Church's welcome pack and on their websites: Miracle Temple Ministries Inc. http://www.miracle-temple-ministries.org/43/index.html; Willesden New Testament Church of God: http://www.wntcg.org.uk/index.htm. In Flatlands Church of God, the men's ministry is called Life Builders Men's Ministry. Documentation of their mission and objectives can be found at http://www.lifebuilders.to/news/?page_id=38.

Another mission perspective that has been perpetuated by the churches in both New York City and London is the focus on 'local' evangelism. However it bears noting that within the New York context in particular the definition of local has become more nuanced in that what was solely an indication of location has also taken on cultural applications, thus 'local' evangelism has also come to signify evangelism specifically to members of the West Indian community who may or may not live in your local community. This nuanced re-definition of 'local' finds its best representation in Miracle Temple Ministries Inc. This ministry has eight branches in three countries. Two branches, including the headquarters in New York City, are in the United States, five are in Jamaica and one branch is in Canada. Miracle Temple's status as an international ministry is documented on the church's sign: "Miracle Temple Ministries, for all Nations", within the literature produced by the ministry, on the ministry's website and is expressed almost every Sunday during the welcome by the founding minister and general overseer of the ministry. However, upon closer investigation it is revealed that the congregation in the churches affiliated with this ministry, though located in various countries, is still predominantly West Indian. So although the ministry has gained an international status in terms of where the branches are located, it is still very much 'local' in the cultural sense in that it primarily reaches out to individuals of a West Indian background. In London by contrast, although certain aspects of this redefinition is in practice, in that the congregation is still predominantly of West Indian ancestry, it is not as prominent. For as West Indian identities have given way to the emergence of Black British identities within the British context, the term 'local' evangelism has reclaimed much of its locational definition. Although other minorities or whites are still a minority in these churches, they are there. Also key measures have been implemented by the leaders of the church to ensure that members of the surrounding community are not excluded. The most notable of these are: discouraging the use of patois; developing a more contemporary style of worship service in terms of the songs and music used as well as the use of multi-media, and the removal of certain restriction placed on dress that had excluded others in past, specifically the use of head covering for women and the wearing of trousers. Today women within the congregation and leadership can attend church and even preach with their heads uncovered and also wear trousers.

Within the New York context, the mission perspectives articulated have remained 'otherworldly' centred, with a gospel that is still primarily about personal salvation. In regards to social activities, the churches continue to focus on welfare services, namely: benevolence ministries, chaplaincy and visiting the sick in the hospitals, and holding daily prayer meetings that are open to the public. By contrast, a hybridization has occurred within the London context that integrates various aspects of an 'otherworldly' and 'this worldly' mindset. So although the evangelism still has a personal salvation focus it also incorporates an active engagement with the surrounding community. This active engagement has taken the following forms: public marches, participation in the 'Not one more drop of blood' anti-crime campaign, joint church meetings to discuss and make community appeals, and the encouragement of members to become actively involved in politics. In Willesden New Testament Church of God, active engagement with the community has resulted in a self-funded community project focused on the needs of pensioners in the surrounding area. Although this project is now organized and funded by the Brent County Council, the activities are still held at the church. In this manner, the church continues to play a vital role in the community.

One area in which both contexts are conceptualizing and practising mission in a new manner is in the use of multi-media and other technologies. Two of the three churches have web pages which according to one informant is another 'means of getting the gospel out'[34]. For all three congregations the potential presented by the use of multi-media in 'spreading the gospel' is indispensable. In Willesden New Testament Church of God in London, many of the hymnals and pew bibles have been replaced by song lyrics and bible verses projected unto an overhead screen and through two television monitors. Although Miracle Temple Ministries Inc. has not gone high tech in terms of using overhead projectors and other multi-media technologies they are already prepared for this. According to an informant 'when... Bishop was erecting the new sanctuary from ground up, ...the wires were run already, everything was put in the ceiling getting ready for this. So the vision was there and that all happened back in 2000 that we would use technology to get the gospel

---

34 Interview with a first generation female member and leader of Miracle Temple Ministries Inc.

90

out.'[35] Within Flatlands Church of God, there is hybridization in that multi-media technology is being used during the Praise and Worship part of the liturgy, while the traditional hymnals and pew bibles are used throughout the rest of the service.

Conclusion

The importance of the mission perspectives articulated and re-formulated within Pentecostal West Indian immigrant churches in the diaspora is paramount. For these perspectives function like signatures, highlighting the process in which the migrants are actively engaged as they navigate between their past, and their present – i.e. taking the faith that shaped them and re-casting it in a fashion that is viable within their current context, while also allowing their current context to dictate, in some respect, what some of these valid options should be. Interlaced within this process are the issues of identity and continuity as the second, third and fourth generation emerges.

---

35 Interview with a first generation female member and leader of Miracle Temple Ministries Inc.

References

Anderson Robert Mapes, *Vision of the Disinherited: The making of American Pentecostalism* (New York: Oxford University Press, 1979)

Beckford Robert, *Dread and Pentecostal: A Political Theology for the Black Church in Britain* (London: Society for Promoting Christian Knowledge, 2000)

Bell Derrick, *Faces at the Bottom of the Well: The Permanence of Racism* (New York: Basic Books, 1992)

Cross Malcolm, and Entzinger Han, eds., *Lost Illusions: Caribbean Minorities in Britain and the Netherlands* (London: Routlege, 1988)

Crowder Kyle D., 'Residential Segregation of West Indians in the New York/New Jersey Metropolitan Area: The Roles of Race and Ethnicity'. *International Migration Review*, Vol. 33 No. 1 (Spring 1999)

Foner Nancy, 'Race and Color: Jamaican Migrants in London and New York City', *International Migration Review*, Vol. 19, No. 4 (Winter 1985)

Jamaican Farewell: Jamaican migrants in London (London: Routledge & Kegan Paul, 1979)

Gordon Shirley C., *God Almighty Make Me Free: Christianity in Preemancipation Jamaica* (Bloomington: Indiana University Press, 1996)

Grant Paul, and Patel Raj, eds., *A Time to Speak: Perspectives of Black Christians in Britain,* (Nottingham: Russell Press, 1990)

Hill Clifford, *Black Churches: West Indian and African Sects in Britain,* (London: Community and Race relations unit of the British Council of Churches, 1971)

Hollenweger Walter J., "After Twenty Years' Research on Pentecostalism," *International Review of Mission 75* Ja (1986)

Jackson Anita, *Catching Both Sides of the Wind: Conversations with Five Black Pastors* (London: The British Council of Churches, 1985)

Jenkins Philip, *The Next Christendom: The Coming of Global Christianity* (New York: Oxford University Press, 2002)

McGrath Alister E., *The Future of Christianity* (Oxford: Blackwell Publishers Ltd, 2002)

MacRobert Iain, *The Black Roots and White Racism of Early Pentecostalism in the USA* (Basingstoke: Macmillan, 1988).

Meissner Doris M., Hormats Robert D., Walker Antonio Garigues, and Ogata Shijuro, *International Migration Challenges in a New Era.* (New York: The Trilateral Commission, 1993)

Mortensen Viggo, 'What is happening to global Christianity?' *Dialog* 43 (1) 2004, pp. 20-27

Phillips Mike, and Phillips Trevor, *Windrush: The irresistible rise of Multi-Racial Britain* (London: HarperCollins Publishers, 1998)

Walls Andrew F., *The Cross-Cultural Process in Christian History* (New York: Orbis Books, 2002)

Waters Mary C., 'Ethnic and Racial Identities of Second-Generation Black Immigrants in New York City'. *International Migration Review*, Vol. 28, No.4, Special Issue: The New Second Generation (Winter, 1994)

West Cornell, *Race Matters*. (Boston: Beacon Press, 1993)

Interviews

Interview with a 1.5 generation male member of Miracle Temple Ministries Inc.

Interview with a first generation African female member of Willesden New Testament Church of God in London.

Interview with a first generation female member and leader of Miracle Temple Ministries Inc.

Websites

Church of God website: http://www.churchofgod.cc/about/church_is.cfm

New Testament Church of God in Jamaica website: http://www.ntcgjaci.org/history.htm.

Miracle Temple Ministries Inc. http://www.miracle-temple-ministries.org/43/index.html

Willesden New Testament Church of God: http://www.wntcg.org.uk/index.htm.

Life Builders Men's Ministry: http://www.lifebuilders.to/news/?page_id=38

Chapter Five

The Hindu Diaspora in the UK:
Insights and Challenges for Christian Mission

Israel Selvanayagam

Boosting Memories

It is not easy to trace the exact historic moment when Hindus started their life and encounter in the United Kingdom. A Hindutva writer[1] mentions ten phases of Christian-Hindu interaction, and the first took place in the Roman Empire in which, on the one hand, 'Hinduism faced a determined assault from Christianity' and on the other hand, 'Greeks had learnt their wisdom from the Brahmans of India'. Although this book brings together some useful information, historians might find some of its historical assumptions highly conjectural and needing substantial evidence.

Raja Rammohun Roy (1772-1833), a great reformer of Hindu India and founder of the Brahmo Samaj, based in Calcutta, represented the Mughal Emperor Akbar Shah II to the East India Company in London in 1831 and was invited there to give evidence before the House of Commons on the problems of Bengal. While British colonists and Christian missionaries based in Serampore claimed to represent a civilisation, Roy's mother insisted that he should take a cow and three helpers including a poor relative and his adopted son with him so that he might not get contaminated by the pollution of British life. When they arrived in Liverpool docks it was national news. He made use of the visit to make connections with the Unitarians who came close to the Brahmo Samaj's beliefs and principles.

---

1 Sita Ram Goel, *Hindu-Christian Encounters – A History*, New Delhi: Voice of India, 1989.

As he was dying of meningitis at Beech House, Stapleton, in Bristol, he most carefully stipulated that he was not to be buried in consecrated ground but to be buried alone and in silence – that is, without Christian prayers or service. On the night of 26th-27th September, 1833, he required his doctors to place him, as a Hindu would be, on the floor of his room. He was discovered to be wearing his Brahmanical sacred thread. His funeral was conducted exactly as he had wished. Such a death and interment would ensure that his reformed Hindu sect, the Brahmo-Samaj, and his business and financial interests, his bequests to his family, and his reputation as an Indian reformer would not suffer posthumous attack. Later, his burial plot and Beech House were sold and his remains interred in Arnos Vale in a new, private, non-conformist cemetery where they still lie under an interesting, mandir style canopy which was designed by William Princep (then of Calcutta) and financed by Prince Dwarkanath Tagore.[2]

For the sake of preserving his tomb there was a campaign to save Arnos Vale from being sold to a housing development. His bust adorns the Council House and the Museum in Bristol to which was added in 1997 the establishment of his statue between the Cathedral and the Council House. Great figures including Rabindranath Tagore, Aurobindo Ghose and Keshab Chander Sen followed Roy's path of visiting Britain without compromising their tradition and culture.

From the Hindu religious point of view the most significant visit to the UK was from Swami Vivekananda (1863-1902). Vivekananda made a great impact by a short speech of greeting to the World's Parliament of Religions in Chicago in 1893, where he appeared to be 'the Hindu spiritual hero' advocating the end of hostilities between religions and claiming Hinduism the world religion of tolerance and harmony. Leaving the Parliament as a celebrity he embarked on a lecture tour in America, collected funds for his Ramakrishna Mission and then did the same in England in 1896, where he founded a Vedanta Society in London. On the one hand he was impressed by the material development of the West, which with necessary correction could be applied to India. And on the other hand, he claimed that the neo-

---

2   Carla Contractor, "Rajah Rammohun Roy (19th Century India's Greatest Citizen?) and his Perspective on Christianity", *Pilgrim*, No. 12 April 1998.

Vedanta he represented had the panacea for the ills of a materialistic society in the West. This included particular type of yoga that helps to control the body and senses and reactivates the inner strength to work for an integrated development of humans and societies. Though his radical interpretation of Vedanta (which matches the later Christian liberation theology) and his ideas for the reformation of Hinduism have been forgotten or concealed, today Hindus project him as the first Hindu missionary to the West.

While Vivekananda was taking the route from India to America and England, Annie Besant, a new convert to the Theosophical Society went from England to America and then to India in 1893. Having divorced her husband, she joined the Fabian Society started by George Bernard Shaw. Attracted to Theosophy while reviewing Madam Blavatsky's book *The Secret Doctrine* she went to India and became an ardent member of the Theosophical Society and fierce critic of the West and Christianity. In a lecture given at the Presidency College, Madras in November 1914, Besant said,

> I came back to the point with which I started: that, after a study of some forty years and more, of the great religions of the world, I find none so perfect, none so scientific, none so philosophical, and none so spiritual as the great religion known by the name of Hinduism. The more you know it, the more you will love it, the more you try to understand it, the more deeply will you value it.[3]

As Sarma observes, 'Her fervour, her eloquence, her energy, her personality and her prestige as a lady belonging to the ruling race as well as her whole-hearted support of the entire edifice of Hinduism and her denunciation of the scientific materialism of the West took the country by storm for several years and led to a wide-spread religious awakening among the Hindus'.[4]

There was a counter-force around this time. Pandita (learned) Ramabai (1858-1922), a convert from Brahmanic Hinduism, daughter of a Brahmin teacher of progressive thinking, widowed by the

---

3   Quoted, D.S. Sarma, *Hinduism Through the Ages*, Bombay: Bharatiya Vidya Bhavan, 1973, pp. 116f.

4   Ibid., p. 117.

untimely death of her husband, a low caste man, was baptised with her only daughter when they were in England. She had almost all the gifts of Besant. Her hearing defect prevented her doing medicine for which she came to England and she was employed by the British Defence Department to teach Marathi to the English army men who were being prepared to go to Maharashtra. On return to India, she established homes for rehabilitating Brahmin widows who had a hell of life, as she describes in her book *The High Caste Hindu Women* (1887). In her international tours she mentioned the plight of such women and other social evils in Indian society. Embarrassed by this, Vivekananda had to counter her claims. Such one-sided projections of the Hindu India continue even today.

Besides these figures one can mention Gandhi, Radhakrishnan and a host of writers, artists, economists and leaders who have made a big impact on thinking within the UK. Their memories live on in the present community of Hindus and give them a sense of pride in the face of distorted propaganda about their cultures and beliefs in the press.

Mass Immigrants and Stable Settlement
According to the 2001 census 559,000 Hindus lived in the UK and today it is estimated this figure has risen to 600,000. After the initial experience of being unwelcomed, ignored and even hated, they have been developing their religious centres which also operate as cultural centres where the sound, smell, style and structures of their homeland are replicated.

Further development of Hinduism in the UK took place in 1960s and 1970s with a large number of Hindu immigrants settling mostly from Africa and India. Of the Hindu population in the UK, up to 70% are Gujarati, up to 15% are Punjabi and the rest are from other parts of India, Sri Lanka and other countries. The majority of the Hindus in the UK speak one or more languages apart from English. These include Gujarati, Hindi, Punjabi, Bengali and Tamil. Sanskrit is greatly used in the religious texts and ceremonies.

'Just over fifty percent of the Hindus in the UK live in London – Harrow and Brent having the largest concentration. Other larger communities are in Leicester, Birmingham and Bradford'[5].

Organisations and Activities

Originally the 'Hindu Cultural Society' with a temple/shrine at the centre was formed in major cities of Hindu concentration such as Bradford.[6] Later Hindu organisations sprang up at national level. There is the National Council of Hindus in the UK. Apart from visiting Gurus, movements such as Hare Krishna, Sai Baba, Art of Living, Ramakrishna Mission, the Theosophical Society and Brahmo Samaj are active. There is great solidarity among the Hindus in spite of their different sects, traditions and distinct identities of origin, as evident from organisations such as National Council of Hindu Temples (established in 1978), to which 144 temples are affiliated so far including the magnificent Swaminarayan Temple in Neasden in London and the Balaji Temple just outside Birmingham. The temple premises function as community and cultural centres promoting language studies, art and literature. There is a UK unit of the World Council of Hindus. As their website notes the 'Hindu Council UK was founded in 1994 for all Hindus domiciled in the United Kingdom, combining all the Hindu faith denominations, whilst representing various Hindu communities and Hindus from different parts of the world settled in the United Kingdom. Its main purpose was to give the UK Hindus an effective voice on policy matters with the Government of the day whilst enhancing mutual understanding among the major faiths predominant in the UK. The National Council of Hindus is itself a non-partisan faith organisation. More recently, the Hindu Forum of Britain has been established to represent Hindus in the UK in government programmes and consultations concerning faith communities. For example, it has been successful in launching 'an enquiry into the identity and public engagement of Hindus in Britain' with the governmental department of Communities and Local Government.[7] There is a growing organisation of Hindu Youth UK

---

5   http://www.nchtuk.org/index.php (1.7.07).

6   David Bowen, "The Hindu Community in Bradford" in *Hinduism in England*, ed. by David Bowen, Bradford: Bradford College, 1981, pp. 40ff.

7 See *Connecting British Hindus*, London: Hindu Forum of Britain (year not given).

based in Leicester. Economically Hindus are said to be doing well and it is significant to note that some of the ten wealthiest persons in the UK are Hindus.

Promotion of Indigenous Culture

While enjoying the advantages of political and economic structures of the UK, Hindus are zealously guarding their cultural identity. Colourful festivals and extravagant public performance of Vedic rituals in the name of world peace and prosperity attract the UK public. Occasionally alarming stories hit the headlines, such as over the statues of bulls in Hindu temples drinking milk (early 90s) and over attempts to protect bulls even if they have infectious diseases such as TB, as in the recent case in a temple in Wales. Most Hindus practise and promote vegetarianism.

The Hindus' adherence to ancient traditions hardly gives any room for flexibility to be influenced by the traditions of the UK. Where other buildings, mostly churches, are converted to temples, the outer structure is kept intact but the inner structure is modified according to the Agamic prescriptions. And conspicuous name boards proclaim the fact that the temple stands in the place of a church. Increasingly, new temples are built according to the Agamic prescriptions from the foundation stone to the dedication of the whole structure. For example, Sri Swaminarayan Temple in Neasden is said to be the first traditional Mandir in Europe. It has involved the following:

> 2,828 tons of Bulgarian limestone and 2,000 tons of Italian Carrara marble were shipped to India, carved by over 1,500 craftsmen and reshipped to London. In all, 26,300 carved pieces were assembled like a giant jigsaw within 3 years.

The temple's website adds that 'It is a miracle in modern times worked by over a thousand volunteers'[8].

Since its opening in August 1995, the Mandir has attracted over 3 million visitors and 2,500 school visits. They come to experience living Hinduism and the peace and tranquillity that the sacred Mandir and murtis provide. Together with the mandir, the 'Understanding

---

8   *Swaminarayan Sanstha: Social & Spiritual Care* (12 sheeted reports and photographs, without date and page number (by count, page 8). (www.swaminarayan.org)

Hinduism' exhibition treats visitors to a concise, yet comprehensive study of the Hindu religion. It is an ideal place to learn about the glorious culture of India and the values of Hindu Dharma.

The Hindu Temple of Shri Venkateswara (Balaji) near Birmingham is the most recent 'miracle' and the first of its kind in Europe and is said to be 'the culmination of deeply felt spiritual aspirations of the Hindus in the United Kingdom'. It is not only a worship place but also a cultural centre for those who are from south India.

This majestic temple is the standing testimony of Chola architecture. The inauguration ceremony of this temple and the installation of Lord Balaji, Shri Padmavathi and Shri Hanuman was held from 23rd to 27th August 2006. The Kumbabishekam and Prana Pradhistapana event attracted more than 25,000 devotees of Lord Venkateswara. More than 400 volunteers from all walks of life worked relentlessly to make this event a great success. 21 priests and Vedic scholars who studied Vaikansa Agama conducted the whole Kumbabishekam. The process of instilling life into the idols is a breathtaking experience.[9]

It was a spectacular event intensely spread over five days with supplementary ritual ceremonies for the following 48 days. During major festivals like Diwali an elaborate ritual takes place for hundreds of business people.[10] One needs some orientation to Vedic religion of ritual sacrifice to have a reasonable grasp of what is happening.

Culturally Apologetic

Being a minority Hindus are very particular about portraying the glory of Hinduism in order to attract the UK public. It is interesting to note that while the Hindus continue to criticise Christians for being Western in India, they expect their white converts to be culturally Indian and Hindu in the UK. Those white converts take up Hindu dress pattern as prescribed in the particular sect or guru movement. Art and music keep up the Indian pattern. Nothing is to be mixed!

---

9   Printed on the back cover of the DVD of the inaugural ceremonies.

10 For pictures and descriptions of what is known as Samuh Chopda/Sharda Puja, see
    Sanatan Sandesh, Shree Sanatan Mandir, Leicester , Diwali (9 Nov., 2007), pp. 40ff.

Although the caste system and its worst outcome - untouchability - has scriptural reference even in the most popular text, the Bhagavad Gita, Hindus in the Diaspora try to interpret it as an aspect of culture while some dare to deny outright the continued existence of untouchability. Following a recognition of the Vedic reference to the creation of four *varnas* (Brahmins, Ksatriyas, Vaisyas and Sudras for respective roles as priests and teachers, rulers and warriors, agriculturists and tradesmen and those of servitude) it is noted:

> Although the Hindu social system of dividing people according to varna is now largely hereditary, the scriptures emphasise that originally a person would be categorised according to personal qualities, rather than by birth. The original system was therefore less rigid, but later it became hereditary with individuals identifying themselves with a hereditary group called jati which are associated with a varna. These jati groups are also referred to as castes and sub-castes, can be used to indicate a person's social responsibility and status, and are mainly used for social activities such as arranged marriages.[11]

It requires a separate study to establish the level and scale of inter-caste dining, temple and worship and marriage among the Hindus in the UK. It has been observed that though division of sub-castes is overcome, on the whole, the 'idiom of caste' and caste consciousness with 'primordial attachment' and 'natural affinity' has not been abolished.[12] The Dalit Hindus in UK are right to ask for proving the Hindu claim of transcending caste by appointing Dalit priests in their temples. It is intriguing that against the expectation that the process of globalisation would abolish caste; in fact the caste is being globalised!

Hindu Theology of Religions

Polytheism in Hindu mythology does not present the peaceful co-existence of gods, and henotheism appeared to represent a step forward, though the conflicts between gods for supremacy could not be avoided. *Tirumurti* or the Indian Triad was a major step in working out the ecumenism of gods according to which the three major gods

---

11   http://www.nchtuk.org/index.php (1.7.07).

12   See Helen Kanitkar, "Caste in Contemporary Hindu Society" in *Hinduism in England*, ed. by David Bowen, Bradford: Bradford College, 1981, pp. 94ff.

Brahma, Vishnu and Siva were attributed respectively the acts of creation, preservation and destruction of the cycles of aeons. But it was short-lived. Later Brahma receded to the background and Siva and Vishnu were accepted by their devotees each as God Supreme who was believed to do all the above acts. It is difficult to establish that both, along with many minor deities, were the manifestations of the same reality, because each tradition has a distinct corpus of scriptures such as Puranas, Agamas and devotional texts. There are stories of competition between the two over supremacy and these are referred to in their respective devotional literature. In the process of myth-making different forms of the Goddess were incorporated into their tradition as the consorts of Siva and Vishnu. Further, many other popular deities were incorporated as avatars in the Vaishnava tradition and members of the divine family in the Saiva tradition. Krishna and Ram are the most famous avatars and Ganesh and Murukan, formerly independent deities, became the sons of Siva and Parvati.

Normally in India in most Hindu temples gods and goddesses of the different traditions do not occupy the same temple. Diverse cults and sects, particularly the major Saiva and Vaishnava traditions are very strong. But in the UK in most temples Saiva and Vaishanava gods are made to sit together comfortably in the forms of marble idols. When asked, the answer is that being a minority in the UK Hindus cannot afford to be sectarian. More glaringly, in the Balaji temple, though Hanuman and Lakshmi (servant and consort) flank the sanctum sanctorum of Vishnu, on either side separate shrines for Ganesh and Karthikeyan (Murukan) have been constructed. The personified divinities of nine planets are established in a hall where there are clear marks of the performance of Vedic rituals. More shrines are expected to be added so that Hindus of different sects, regions and traditions can come together in one premises and worship. There are separate priests for the Vaishnava and Saiva shrines.

It is interesting to note that during the dedication of the Balaji temple the theme mentioned in the speeches was 'unity is divinity' and the same words form the title of the DVD of the spectacular performance of rituals. Cultural events are organised such as dance, concerts and musical discourses.

Historically, at least in South India, the Jainas and Buddhists were considered the archenemy of the Vaishanva and Saiva traditions. But in the UK Buddhism and Jainism are often regarded as part of Hinduism. Jaina Mahavira and Gautama Buddha were fierce critiques of the extravagant ritual practices of the Vedic religion. Later, Buddha was taken as one of the avatars of Vishnu. If mass conversion from Hinduism to Islam and Christianity happens in India Hindus in the UK make a hue and cry, but when Hindus become Buddhists they are somewhat calmer. But there is difficulty in accommodating Buddhism today because of the neo-Buddhist movement, pioneered by the champion of Dalit liberation, which is very critical of Brahmanic Hinduism.

The Rig Vedic verse 'Truth is One and the wise call it differently' has been repeated by Hindus as their golden verse for understanding one God or Reality and different manifestations within and even other religions without. I have shown elsewhere how the verse is taken out of context (where the 'Truth' is most probably a mysterious magnificent altar) and used to upset those (particularly Muslims and Christians) who approach them with one Truth and one Religion.[13] Without recognising the irreconcilable differences both within and without, Hindus of all types, ranging from philosophers to poor masses, find it intellectually convincing and spiritually attracting to say that ultimately there is only one God, the creator and father of all beings. Just as there can be many photographs of one sun, many pathways to the same hilltop and many streams joining the same sea, for them, all religions are moving towards or cohering around one God or Reality. This is in spite of hair-splitting debates within their philosophical schools about the existence and nature of God in which refuting the claims of others is tolerated. The difference between plurality or diversity and contradiction is the most important issue that Hindus have to come to terms with.

Mission and Service

From running hospitals to helping the victims of natural calamities, combined with spiritual teachings and yogic exercises, Hindus through

---

13 I. Selvanayagam, *The Dynamics of Hindu Religious Traditions: The Teape Lectures on Sacrifice, Gita and dialogue*, Bangalore: Asian Trading Corporation, 1996, pp. 98ff.

their temple organisations are engaged in social and spiritual service. It is not difficult to notice their imitation of Christian models of mission and service, not least in running Sunday Schools. 'Art of Living in the UK' is the name of a guru movement which aims to teach spirituality to the citizens of the UK most of whom are in their view fed up with a consumerist culture and nominal religious life.

While they welcome Christian conversion to Hinduism and even condone re-conversion back to Hinduism, as is happening in India, they vehemently attack those 'predatory religions' who try to convert someone from one religion to another. There is a considerable Hindu lobby against any form of religious conversion in international forums. Is it the expression of enormous tolerance and an inclusive outlook or fear of losing their flock?

More recently, there are efforts to gain limelight for Hindu involvement in economic transformation at world level. In 'A Shared Vision for Reducing World Poverty – British Government and British Hindus Working to Realise the Common Good' the following statements appear:

> Shouldn't it be our moral and religious duty, our *Dharma*, to ensure that we are part of a world where no one has to live in poverty? A world in which all have access to food, shelter, clean water; to a livelihood, health and education. A world in which the rights and dignity of every woman, man and child to live life to the full are respected.

This is the vision that inspires the work of the UK Government Department for International Development (DFID) and many charities and aid agency affiliates of 'Hindu Aid'. For Hindus, serving humanity is like serving God, and it is the duty of Hindus to give their service in whichever way they can as a form of worship. Thus it is imperative that the whole of humanity is accorded the means to a dignified livelihood. Target 2015 is in keeping with this vision.

This vision is not a dream – we believe that it could be a reality. The world's governments, including our own, are playing a key role in the realisation of this dream, with their agreement to an ambitious campaign to cut by half the proportion of people who live in absolute poverty by 2015.[14]

One can appreciate easily how in this publicity booklet with pictures and captions ideas and programmes are implicitly shared with other agencies such as Christian Aid and Islamic Relief. Also Hindus often play a leading role in drawing the attention of the UK government to the feelings of the minority religious communities. The recent 'Faith Community Consultation Consortium' in its response to the introduction of identity cards is an example.[15]

Hindu-Christian Dialogue in the UK

Christian study of Hinduism and identification of issues in Christian-Hindu dialogue has a long history. Whether Hindus have been taken as equal partners in dialogue in all the attempts is a question. In any case, not many Hindus are around who are aware of this long history. This is a real drawback for creating a sustained Hindu-Christian dialogue today.

Apart from small local interfaith groups in which Hindus are represented mainly in civic celebrations and individual cases of interfaith friendship I am not aware of any Hindu-Christian dialogue taking place in the UK. It was in 2004 the Hindu-Christian Forum in the UK was formed by a group of Hindus and Christians meeting alternatively between Leicester and Watford Junction. From the beginning there was the problem of getting a consistent number of representatives from both sides. Despite hot debates on sharing of 'faith' (Hindu preference was 'tenets') and conversion, a 'Statement of Goodwill' was achieved. Though there was a decision not to bring issues from India it almost proved to be unavoidable. There was only one session fully devoted to an understanding and interpretation of scriptures. Because of the immense variety of Hindu scriptures, both primary and secondary, getting a comprehensive view was not possible. Issues of caste and conversion were like tinderboxes waiting for friction and flame, which were carefully avoided.

---

14 *Target 2015 Halving Poverty: Hindu Aid*: Hindu Aid/DFID Publications, UK (year not given).

15 *Summary of the Consultation with Faith Communities in Britain*, England: Fujitsu Services Limited and the Faith Community Consultation Forum, 2005.

The constituency of Hindus changed few times. Finally, the forum has been reconstituted in a big meeting held in London. The Secretary General of the Hindu Forum of Britain has promised to raise the profile of the Hindu-Christian Forum and of initiating dialogue on issues of mutual interest.

In the meantime, the visit of Archbishop Rowan Williams to the main Hindu Temple (*Sanatana* Mandir) in Leicester in 2005 provided a new impetus for Hindu-Christian dialogue. The Archbishop while appreciating the new initiative of Hindu-Christian Forum, urged the group to move into deeper theological issues with a view to finding common ground and difference on which further dialogue could continue. There is a planning group working on a theological conference which the Archbishop has agreed to address.

Insights and Challenges for Christian Mission

In the name of community cohesion and interfaith integration the British government through appropriate departments and local councils pump in grants but as far as one observes everything except faith is talked about. Unless there is commitment to explain their faith and understand other faiths interfaith integration and harmony will continue to be elusive. Hindus and Christians have a long way to go to achieve minimum understanding of each other's faith, traditions and interpretations.

As scholars have observed, Hindus always appear to 'christianise' their faith. They hardly claim the uniqueness of their faith. But the rituals performed with appropriate recitations in Sanskrit by priests in Hindu temples are very unique. There is a strong belief in the intrinsic power of ritual and even gods or God have to depend on the ritual performances for their life and sustenance. But informed Hindus have ready-made answers which compare their ritual power to the Catholic doctrine of transubstantiation of bread and wine becoming the body and blood of Christ in Holy Communion. Moreover, although there have been protestant movements within Hinduism which have denounced idol worship, those who worship idols do not recognise it. It is difficult to explain to them the difference between idols, icons and symbols.

Accepting Jesus as one of the great teachers or incarnations is not at all a problem for Hindus. Creation stories, mythical stories of divine activities and ethical teachings are abundant in Hinduism. They have to be told the whole gospel story, starting from God's choice of a slave community to be the instrument and model of God's humanising or saving mission, the struggle between God's love and justice as portrayed in the prophetic literature, the distinctive uniqueness of the Jewish Jesus who came to be seen as the cosmic Christ, the cost of Christian discipleship in response to God's love in Christ through worship and service, and the joy of hope for a new heaven and new earth as the basic ingredients of the gospel. These are yet to be shared and understood. God's unconditional acceptance of any person for a new orientation and purpose in life without any burden to be carried for the future in this life or the next life can be really good news to be reaffirmed by Christians and shared with Hindus with respect, courtesy and gentleness.

Chapter Six

Non-western Christian missionaries in England: Has mission been reversed?

Rebecca Catto

This chapter draws on research conducted over the course of my doctoral project in the sociology of religion which was designed as an investigation into 'reverse mission' - hence the title of this chapter. Data was gathered using qualitative methods: principally semi-structured interviewing and participant observation. In this chapter I will provide a provisional answer to the question posed by the title - firstly by discussing the background to the notion of 'reverse mission', including consideration of geographical divisions. The issue will then be illuminated through empirical illustrations drawn from my own research, which lead in turn to a conclusion emphasising the complexity of the overall picture.

Background to the notion

'Reverse mission', 'mission in reverse', 'mission in return' are now familiar phrases. They have grown up in Christian missionary circles in the late 20th century. They are shorthand for an historical shift, with Christian missionaries now coming from countries that were traditionally receivers of mission to work in countries which traditionally were senders of missionaries. Philip Jenkins in his well-known and provocative book *The Next Christendom* writes "We can even imagine Southern Christians taking the initiative to the extent of evangelising the North..." (2002:14). Grace Davie in her 2002 book *Europe: The Exceptional Case* writes of how 'mission in reverse' would turn the traditional relationship between Africa and Europe on its head. However, she also states that this hasn't happened yet (Davie 2002:110). Adogame and Weissköppel make reference to "This new 'reverse-mission' initiative…" (2005:6) in relation to African Christian movements.

In addition to growing academic attention, the notion has received considerable media attention. An Indian Christian minister working in England is referred to as a reverse missionary in a February 2005 article from the Religious News Service. BBC Journalist Naomi Wellings, who has interviewed some of my own respondents, has written of Africa as the 'Light Continent' and how while in the 19th century missionaries from Britain set out on arduous journeys to Africa, today roles seems to be reversed with many Africans hoping to revive interest in Christianity within the land that first brought their grandparents into the church (Wellings internet accessed 25/01/06). Thus we see that the idea most certainly exists, and is applied in both academia and the media, and even to some of my respondents.

However, in her 1984 article in the *International Review of Mission*, Claude Marie Barbour presents a different idea of 'mission-in-reverse'. For Barbour, 'mission-in-reverse' is an approach in which ministers can and should learn from the people ministered to, particularly the poor and marginalised. This interpretation is picked up by Bevans and Schroeder in their 2006 magnum opus on the theology of mission *Constants in Context*. They cite St Francis of Assisi's seven days spent in dialogue with the Egyptian sultan during the Crusades as an example of the approach and attitude today called 'mission in reverse' (2006:143,170). Hence we see that not only are there variations on the term, but also variations of meaning. Yet, the general notion of the historical shift outlined above predominates.

Geographical Divisions
The earlier quotation from Philip Jenkins highlights the fact that talk of 'reverse mission' is situated within discussion about the well-documented demographic shift of Christianity from the global North to the global South. Lammin Sanneh writes "Preindustrial primal societies in the Southern Hemisphere have become major Christian centres" (2005:3). The general characterisation is that the number of Christians is growing in the global South whilst Christian participation declines in the global North, therefore Christians are coming from South to North. Drawing geographical boundaries is fraught with

problems. I have just made reference to the North/South divide. Yet, the abstract for the BIAMS 2007 'Strangers in our midst' conference out of which this book grew made reference to "churches in the West today". This illustrates the abiding strength of the concept of "the West" which is not synonymous with the global North. Consequently, I apply the term 'non-western' to the Christian missionaries I have worked with. The term implies issues of power and colonialism. In *Orientalism* Edward Said emphasises the indissoluble relationship between labelling and power, which is something a western researcher needs to be very conscious of.

We have seen that Wellings focuses on African Christians conducting mission, as do Adogame and Weissk.ppel, and Davie. This highlights the postcolonial aspect of 'reverse mission' with Christians from former colonies coming to work in Europe.

My own research has involved interviews with people from Nigeria and Kenya, yet I use the term 'non-western' because respondents are also from Latin America, India, Melanesia, South Korea and the Crimea. It is not only difficult to draw geographical distinctions, but distinctions between activities of respondents as well: between mission and ministry, for example. In my doctoral research I have worked with individuals on missionary visas connected to mission societies and with ministers to diaspora congregations. I was guided by self-ascription: whether an individual considered him or herself to be a missionary or not.

Having contextualised the data, we can now move on to look at the reality of my respondents' experiences and how they shed light on our principle question.

Empirical Illustrations

The case of the Melanesian Brothers and Sisters may be taken as a textbook example of 'reverse mission'. They are members of Anglican religious communities in Melanesia, which is a former British colony. The Anglican Church was founded in Melanesia over one hundred and fifty years ago by Bishop Patteson from the Exeter Diocese. In 2005 a group of Brothers and Sisters participated in a three month mission to the UK spending time in Chester, Exeter and London. One brother told me how they were there to show the fruits of Bishop Patteson's mission by coming back to England. Another spoke of Bishop Patteson's sacrifice (he was killed in Melanesia), and the fact that they are now here on mission to help – in other words to strengthen the faith.

When I asked respondents in interviews about 'reverse mission', and the applicability of the term to their own work, most were familiar with the term. Responses are illuminating. For example, an Anglican from Kenya working in a deprived English community, said: "we should just be missionaries, not reverse... but a pattern had been set that missionaries go from wealthy countries to the poor countries, from the North to the South.". An Anglican minister from Nigeria commented on 'reverse mission':

"Reverse, yeah... I think it's a good term, and I think it exists, and I think it's happening. You see, when Christianity came to Africa, particularly to my country, from the efforts of the European people that brought the Gospel, and because of that, the average Nigerian Christian is ever grateful for the sacrifice of the European, and particularly, of the British, for bringing the Gospel... I was really touched when I came to this country to see the development in this country, and, within that context, people willingly left, abandoned their place, left their comfort zones... you may call it, and came to Africa... Some came to my own village in a remote part where there were no motorable roads, and some lived around that area doing the mission work and so coming back here now ... touched me, the sacrifice, so some are very conscious of that. And, what is happening today, to me, I think the fruits of their labour is what I call the 'reverse mission'. People are coming over, and they are coming over with a sense you know, to reach out and evangelise and bring mission...".

Yet he is less prepared to apply the phrase to his own work as a minister to Nigerian Christians in London:

"what has not happened properly is for our people to be engaged with the indigenous people in real mission work. What has been happening in some places now has been people coming over from there and reaching out to their own people, just like what we are doing...".

112

Another Nigerian is a pastor who founded his own Baptist Pentecostal congregation in the North West. When I asked him about reverse mission he said:

> "God used the white people... I'm sorry I'm using the word 'white people', because I don't want to limit it to just the English people, because He used the Americans, and God used them then to bring, to open the eyes... of the Africans, to bring forth the light. For God is now using the same people that He has used the forefathers of these people to bless to come back to bless this generation. So I see God using us really... to bless this generation, but ... it's not that I don't agree with the word 'reverse mission', ok? But... I just see God working in the mysterious ways, the ways that are pleasing to Him to work. So we Africans are, we are doing a lot of work now though people claim that British are losing, they are losing the plot spiritually, but God is using us...".

The question arises: who is a reverse missionary? We see from the quotes from interviews reproduced above that it is a label not unequivocally accepted by individuals to whom one might wish to apply it. It is interesting that the Anglican minister views real mission as involving outreach to indigenous people whereas further on in our interview the Baptist Pentecostal pastor spoke of himself as a missionary though he ministers to a congregation which is approximately ninety percent African.

Respondents offered various interpretations of mission. The frequent refrain was that it is not simply about 'bums on seats'. It is about being with people, setting a good example, and social justice which in fact fits with Barbour's interpretation of 'mission in reverse'. I got the impression that the British context is quite a difficult one in which to conduct missionary work. Respondents complained about not being able to use the same methods that they would at home or to be so direct and open with people. For example, the Baptist Pentecostal pastor continued to say:

> "Take for... instance, in Africa you can just stand on the street and start preaching the Gospel... you can't do that here. I can't remember how many times by the grace of God I've preached

on the bus. I can't try that here can I? No, because they say it's not allowed."

This situation is often attributed to the secular state of Britain. Above we saw the pastor say that Britons are said to be losing the plot spiritually. The Anglican minister from Nigeria mentioned being surprised by the lack of belief he found in what he had expected to be a Christian country. Some Melanesian Brothers noted the lack of young people in churches in Britain. One told me that he thinks that young people in Britain don't go to church because they have too many distractions like computer games and mobile phones. Another Anglican Kenyan missionary said that part of his reason for coming on mission to Britain was to learn from Europe's mistakes and avoid losing the younger generation in Kenya: prevention rather than cure. Certainly Europe is perceived as in need of mission - an Indian respondent said "the whole continent needs to be re-evangelised".

Many of my respondents were invited to do mission work by British missionary organisations, and part of the motivation behind the invitation does seem to be a desire to learn from their relative success. An English Anglican instrumental in bringing the Melanesian Brothers and Sisters to England said part of the motivation for the mission was reinvigorating Christians in England. Indeed, most of the Melanesian Brothers and Sisters' activities were with people from within the Anglican Church rather than outreach to unchurched populations - something some respondents have been trying to do and have found very challenging. From my research, it seems the impact so far of these missionaries on the wider population in England is quite limited. The point that many were invited points up the unequal power relations enduring between the West and the global South: the financial strength abides in the West and consequently so does much control of mission. The missionaries coming from the global South to the West are not coming with the same degree of power and authority as those missionaries who were sent out from Europe during the colonial era.

My respondents are not explicit economic migrants or refugees. Most migrated temporarily for the express purpose of conducting missionary work in Britain. I would question whether they should be described as "strangers in our midst", because many respondents are members of the Anglican Church, and all are members of historic, mission churches. Therefore at least in one sense they are insiders, yet in terms of nationality, and ethnicity, they are 'other'. The Baptist Pentecostal pastor from Nigeria's consciousness of skin colour has already been seen in his discussion of white people having brought the Gospel to the forefathers of Africans. Some missionaries told me about how they use their 'otherness' as a tool for mission. People are curious, and consequently it is a way to start a conversation. Some also spoke of racism encountered. Thus we see that the status of respondents in England is difficult, and needs to be managed carefully. They are concomitantly insiders and outsiders made conscious of difference by the contrasting context in which they find themselves. In sum, mission in England is far from easy.

Conclusion

Having learned something of the experiences of individuals who could be labelled as reverse missionaries, let us return to the original question: has mission been reversed?

Something does seem to have changed with members of historic, mission churches founded in their home countries by British missionaries seeing a need for mission in Britain. According to an Anglican Kenyan missionary: "they need more people coming from overseas, because they've been always thinking of sending missionaries, sending, sending, but maybe they are losing the point...".

As part of my research, I have conducted discourse analysis of Church Mission Society newsletters, through which one can trace a shift in consciousness over the course of the 20th century. In the May 1974 CMS Newsletter John V. Taylor writes '20% of the entire population of Kenya attend Christian services regularly every Sunday, and 38% attend church at least once a year. It is a very long time since the figures in Britain were so high.' He goes on to mention the 'unexpected strength of Africa's allegiance to Christianity...' (Taylor 1974:2).

In a more recent newsletter from 1996 Diana Witts reports on a meeting of the Anglican Communion in the United States:

From South America, the Caribbean, all over Africa, and across Asia, we heard exciting stories of dynamic evangelism and rapidly growing churches. From North America, Western Europe and Australasia came reports of a very different kind; giving an overall picture of churches struggling to stem a decline in numbers. What was so striking about these reports was that the normal donor/receiver, rich/poor pattern of churches was reversed (Witts 1996:2).

Nonetheless, I think to claim mission has been reversed is oversimplistic. Though in smaller numbers than previously, Christian missionaries are still sent out from Europe all over world. Also, the situation was never so straightforward historically. Bevans and Schroeder (2006) remind us of the varied and complex patterns of Christian mission over the centuries - Christianity was in Africa before it was in Europe. Only from the1500s onwards did Europe become a missionary sending continent, a shift connected with the rise of colonialism. Christianity has been a missionary religion since its inception. In some ways, therefore, what my respondents are doing is nothing new. There is both continuity and change.

Both distinctive and new, however, is the rate of technological development over the 20th century, which is linked to the process of globalisation of which colonialism is often seen as a precursor. Increasing international contact and travel enable missionaries to communicate and move more swiftly across the globe (though movement may be hampered by national border controls - many respondents reported difficulty with obtaining visas for the UK). Yet, missionaries from these traditionally receiving countries in the global South are not going just to the global North. They are going to other countries in the Southern Hemisphere too. At the same time, many American missionaries come to Europe, Polish Catholics are swelling congregations in England, and so forth. Perhaps then it is better to talk about mission 'from everywhere to everywhere' rather than 'reverse mission' as Diana Witts proceeds to do in her CMS newsletter referenced, and which some respondents advocate. Having said this, though 'from everywhere to everywhere' captures something of globalising processes and the related complexity of contemporary Christian mission, and may be an ideal, it discounts discerning difference and more specific trends/patterns. Therefore, the concept is analytically empty and inadequate.

To conclude, there does seem to be an increasing number of Christians from the global South coming to Europe and conducting mission here. I found a similar thing happening in Sweden with the Church of Sweden's 'Mission in return' project (Harmansson 1999), and similar developments have been documented in the Netherlands and Germany by ter Haar and Adogame respectively. Yet, numbers are still relatively small (and extremely difficult to estimate) and the future hard to predict. The pastor in my sample sees more Christian missionaries coming from all over the globe to do mission in Britain, as do others. One said "the future is going to be like bringing, bringing...", and another told me: "I see myself as one of the early missionaries from the two thirds world... but there will be many, many more coming up behind me, waves and waves." So even though I do not see mission as having been reversed as yet, it may be. With this in mind, the notion of 'reverse mission' is not completely invalidated: it captures an observable and growing trend.

Bibliography

Adogame, A. and Weisskӧppel, C. (eds) 2005 *Religion in the Context of African Migration*, Bayreuth African Studies Series no 75. Bayreuth: Bayreuth University.

Barbour, C M 1984 'Seeking Justice and Shalom in the City', *International Review of Mission*, vol. 73 no. 291, 303-309.

Bevans, S. B. and Schroeder, R. P. 2006 *Constants in Context: A Theology of Mission for Today.* New York: Orbis Books.

Davie, G. 2002 *Europe: the Exceptional Case: Parameters of Faith in the Modern World.* London: Darton, Longman and Todd Ltd.

Harmansson, M. 1999 *Mission i retur: Ett inslag i Svenska kyrkans mission.* Uppsala: Svenska Institutet för Missionsforskning.

Jenkins, P. 2002 *The Next Christendom: the Coming of Global Christianity.* Oxford: Oxford University Press.

Kennel-Shank, C. 2005 'Reversing Historic Model, Missionary from Global South Evangelizes West', *Religion News Service*, 22nd February, 1-2.

Sanneh, L. 2005 'Introduction' in *The Changing Face of Christianity: Africa, the West and the World*, edited by L. Sanneh and J. A. Carpenter, 3-18. New York: Oxford University Press.

Said, E. W. 2003 (1978) *Orientalism*. London: Penguin Books.

Taylor, J. V. 1974 *CMS Newsletter*, no 381. London: CMS.

ter Haar, G. 1998 *Halfway to Paradise: African Christians in Europe*. Cardiff: Cardiff Academic Press.

Witts, D. K. 1996 *CMS Newsletter*, no 529. London: CMS.

Internet resources
Wellings, N www.bbc.co.uk/religion/religions/christianity/features/light_continent/ accessed 25/01/06.

Chapter Seven

Mission and Home-Making: Church Expansion through Migration in the Democratic Republic of Congo

Emma Wild-Wood

I was born in this church, I grew up in this church... it's my home, I can't leave to go to another house, or keep changing to find another place because there is only one faith. Anglicans see themselves a bit like refugees when in other churches.[1]

This is one response to questions of *intent* I wish to ask in this chapter: How do Christian migrants express their faith? Why do they establish churches? Do they think that church expansion through migration is mission? Munege Kabarole, who gave this response, was an evangelist and later archdeacon who helped establish several Anglican Churches for migrant workers in the Democratic Republic of the Congo. He expressed the intent of his work in terms of creating home away from home.

Beyond Congo there is a growing awareness of the role of Christianity (and other faiths) in stimulating migration, supporting immigrant communities and influencing the host culture. Such reflections are often made in the context of cross-continental migration. Considering the *intent* of migrant Christians when they establish churches in new places highlights the agency of migrants and their complex motivations and aspirations. It also allows one to see what was unintended or assumed. Studying intercontinental migration in Africa and examining the relationship between mission and migration on a particular group of migrants who remain on their continent of origin gives insights and models that may provide a

---

1   Munege Kaberole, Bunia

framework for understanding wider movements. Before embarking on this, however, a word on 'mission' is necessary.

One might argue, with David Bosch, that 'mission remains undefinable...the most we can hope for is to formulate some *approximations* of what mission is all about:'[2] ultimately the *missio dei* continues beyond the intentions and definitions of the church. We can, however, suggest that Christian mission, inspired by God's own sending forth, has the intention of showing the love of God in Jesus Christ to the world beyond its own boundaries. Historically, this has often been connected with a move of Christianity into new geographical and cultural areas. Was this the primary intention of Anglican Christians in Congo as their church expanded into new geographical areas?

Background

The Anglican Church of Congo has grown significantly through routes of migration, which on a global scale, are often considered unremarkable. The Church was founded in 1896 by the Ugandan evangelist (and later, priest), Apolo Kivebulaya. He operated within a sixty-mile radius from the mission station at Boga, among the Hema people and those with whom they had client relations. The church remained tiny, rural and isolated until the 1960s when political independence provided greater religious freedom and more opportunities for economic migration. Members moved to towns for education and business and formed new Anglican congregations. Civil unrest also influenced the expansion of the church. In the 1970s, 1980s and 1990s Sudanese, Ugandan, Rwandan and Burundian refugees all played a part in establishing Anglican congregations in Congo. Migration has played a vital part in the expansion of the Anglican church throughout Congo, and indeed, of many other denominations in Africa. The primary intentions of Anglican migrants in planting new churches can, I believe, be broadly split into three groups, which revolve around the importance of a sense of home, or belonging. I have called these intentions 'creating home', 're-ordering home' and 'being homeless'.

---

2   Bosch, David, *Transforming Mission*, Orbis, 1991: 9.

Recreating Home

Many who *chose* to migrate - rather than those forced to flee war - were influenced in their decision by their Christian faith. The Anglican Church promoted education, bio-medicine and monetary employment as signs of God-given improvement. These became more widely available larger, urban centres than in rural areas. Committed church members who were also traders, teachers, students, or even the chronically ill, moved to new places, gathered together and sent home for a church worker to minister to them.

In this situation the multiplication of Anglican congregations provided a familiar form of church life and worship to those in a strange place. Their attachment to the Anglican Church provided them with a sense of home and helped them maintain their ethnic identity and culture. Rwakaikara André, originally from Boga, said this about the Anglican Church that had been established in the town in which he worked, I was born in this church, so I love this church that I was born in. And when we saw it had come here we were happy because people must love the home and the place of their father, of their parents.[3]

People likened their affiliation to a church since birth to remaining in the same home. One may have moved house and settled in town but attachment to one's place of origin was expressed in a religious affiliation that the comfort and familiarity expected of 'home'. As Munege mentioned in the earlier quotation, those used to the Anglican Church felt displaced in other denominations. The very fact that all denominations were seen to be preaching the same essential message made nonsense of permanently joining a different church. Replicating the church from home, in order to feel at home was the priority. In this sense the word 'home' is not being used metaphorically when referring to church. Rather 'home' has a conceptually wide spatial and emotional reach that includes church. Maintaining the faith is necessary in order to develop a sense of belonging in new circumstances.

The aim of this approach is the multiplication of congregations to support members in the faith, offer care, and encourage the conservation of their particular group identity in a new place. The

---

3   Rwakaikara André, Bunia, 23/09/00.

emphasis is on preservation of a tradition. The name of Apolo Kivebulaya, now regarded as a saint, was often invoked to preserve the Anglican tradition that had developed a close relationship with Hema culture and people. Little attention was given to stepping beyond the familiar structural and cultural boundaries that had been established in a different place. There was a tendency to exclusivity and ethnocentricity. Although the Anglican Church had never been the preserve of one ethnic group in Congo, the Hema had dominated its leadership. Because of the connection between Christianity and education they were also able to take advantage of migration opportunities. And so in some areas the migrant churches perpetuated this dominance and for a generation the Anglican Church was sometimes called the 'Hema' church.

It has been noted of other migrant groups that familiar customs can become more prominent in a new place that they had been in the original location. A study of the Cherubim and Seraphim in the UK highlighted that the influence of rites and cultural expectations from Nigeria increased as congregations became better established. [4] The priorities of mutual support and a cohesive identity in order to aid the migration process are often in tension with a missional approach that wishes to widen boundaries of inclusion.

It would be unfair to suggest, however, that mission is entirely ignored by those recreating home in a new place. Anglicans in Congo emphasise the importance of activities usually considered part of mission. They speak of 'evangelism' as spreading the Gospel, 'pastoral care' as looking out for other members of the congregation and 'development' in the provision of social services like schools, clinics and agricultural projects. They are public about their faith. Indeed, constructing a church building rather than worshipping in the home of a migrant was understood as a move from the private to the public, of giving others an opportunity to know about them and to join. For example, those who made for themselves a 'home' in Anglicanism expected to see people from their new location benefiting from the schools they established. Nevertheless, any missional success was often confined to a deepening sense of the importance of religious faith

---

4   Frieder Lugwig, 'The Proliferation of Cherubium and Seraphim Congregations in Great Britain,' in Afe Adogame and Cordula Wiessköppel, *Religion in the Context of African Migration*, Bayreuth University Press, 2005, 349.

among the migrants themselves. In other parts of the world this trend to be most effective amongst those of the same cultural background has been observed. Jan Jongeneel writing from the Dutch context calls it 'internal mission'. It does not immediately engage with the host culture but sees dynamic expansion among its own group as migration encourages a re-assessment of faith commitment.[5]

Re-ordering Home

Establishing 'home' in a new place is not desirable to all. In the Anglican Church of Congo various groups had reason to break with tradition. Young women and second-generation migrants wanted to challenge the sense of 'home' that the first migrants desired for their church. Traditions of formal liturgy and quiet music were unappealing and they were connected in the minds of these people with particular expectations of behaviour from young people and women, imposed by their traditional elders. In the 1970s Rwakaikara's daughter, Irene Bahemuka, was critical of the Anglican Church her parents liked so much. She understood the village values differently to her father and accused it of being ethnocentric, formal and unfriendly. She remained within the church, however, and encouraged moves to make the church appear more contemporary and urban. Migrant churches often became the site of a generational struggle to define the identity of the Anglican church. Many of those who challenged the relationship between 'home' and 'church' were second generation migrants. The rural home of their parents did not stretch psychologically into their own location. If church was to be included in their definition of 'home' it had to develop a more urban identity. Generational issues have also been observed in cross-continental migrant churches. In the US second generation immigrants have been observed to be uncomfortable with the ethnic ambience of their parents' religion. They draw on a hybrid range of socio-religious influences, altering their cultural, linguistic and spiritual references to accommodate their present location. [6]

---

5 Jongeneel, Jan A B., 'The mission of Migrant Churches in Europe,' *Missiology*, 31.1. 2003: 29-33.

6 Helen Rose Ebaugh and Janet Saltzman Chafetz, *Religion and the New Immigrants: Continuities and Adaptations in Immigrant Congregations*, (Waltnut Creek: AltaMira), 2000: 129-130.

In the 're-ordering home' model migrant churches were more concerned with internal affairs than in a missional approach beyond their walls. However, the women and young people often expressed their challenge as a desire to be more inclusive of others rather than exclusive, to shape a church which others might want to join. They wanted to adopt forms of worship they saw in other churches, and to meet with other women's groups or youth fellowships.

Another group who re-ordered home were those profoundly affected by the dislocation of migration itself, particularly when the migration had been forced through war. In the North East corner of Congo Anglican congregations began to appear from 1979 as a result of Ugandan refugees fleeing with Idi Amin at the end of his ignominious rule. Those who suffered the most severe dislocation in terms of imprisonment, loss of status, and loss of economic stability often became church leaders and chapel builders. The circumstances of their migration caused them to reassess their life and develop a greater seriousness about their Christian faith. Christian faith was a support and sustenance in the dislocation of migration.

A number of these men established up to fifteen congregations each by visiting villages where they knew there were refugees or plantation workers who had lived in Uganda, and encouraging them to start an Anglican Church. In this case the relationship to 'home' was less obvious. Many of the refugees from Uganda were actually Congolese and had been taking advantage of the better life in Uganda. When they returned 'home' they did not feel 'at home'. Rather they wanted connections with 'abroad'. Some hoped that the Anglican Church would bring them the development advantages and status they had experienced in Uganda. To do this properly it had to improve daily life. Re-ordering home included an emphasis on small-scale development for the local community and a desire to be credible in that community. This did expand the church beyond the migrant population. Among these migrants the primary intentions were mixed but the complex migrant identities of this group encouraged a desire to explore beyond the boundaries of Anglican, ethnic or national senses of belonging.

Being Homeless

A minority of Anglicans drew from their migratory experiences a particular form of mission. It was perhaps a narrow form of mission but it was very intentional. The Congolese Anglican Church has amongst its members a small minority of East African revivalists. Many of these are radical revivalists who have not always maintained communion with mainstream revivalists. Drawing on their revivalism and their migration they developed an understanding of Christian faith which emphasised a sort of homelessness for the Gospel. Home was ultimately a heavenly one. None of them were entirely homeless, but they eschewed worldly possessions, education and agricultural development as distractions from the urgent task of evangelism. They often disregarded their home and preferred to be itinerant or semi-itinerant evangelists.

Revivalism enabled them to redefine the importance of home and of migration. Their forced migration from Congo during the Simba rebellion (1965) and from Uganda during Amin's downfall (1979) was perceived to be part of God's greater purpose. This encouraged them to journey across national, ethnic or just parish boundaries at the prompting of the Holy Spirit. The freedom gained through salvation was perceived to include the freedom to travel in order to preach the gospel, the freedom to detach themselves from thoughts of home, of comfort and security. Status and development were considered worldly vanities. They used their migratory networks to further their evangelism. They insisted that mobility came with faith, as Uketi Amos explained,

> My faith has given me strength to explore lots of unknown places. When I was saved I went by foot to Aru, everywhere... yesterday I was in Nebbi, Uganda. Following this faith I don't worry about my tiredness.[7]

The discourse of tireless itineration was a frequent one among revivalists. They talked of overcoming check-points, border officials and language barriers to preach the Gospel. They criticised other Christians who 'rested' inside churches, rather than striving to promote salvation, frowning on those who made much of creating a spiritual

---

7   Uketi Amos, 29/08/00.

home. In turn, many other Christians found their radical lifestyle and persistent evangelism embarrassingly uncomfortable. Anglican revivalist migrants stressed the verbal proclamation of the Gospel, thus narrowing down what was included in the public, Christian domain. They did gain converts but they remained a fringe group, largely because their aspirations didn't fit with other migrants or the culture around them.

Mission and Migration

The expansion of the Anglican Church of Congo was a result – to a great extent – of the migration of its members. Its migratory growth provides a model of intent and outcome in its expansion. Anglicans had three possible broad objectives when they established new migrant congregations. They aimed to recreate home, re-order home or, in a few radical cases, they adopted a stance of being homeless. Usually migration and the establishment of new congregations were not primarily acts of intentional mission. Both of these, however, were influenced by the public nature of the migrants' Christian faith. Whilst the majority of members were focusing on providing internal support for themselves, they were unintentionally missional because of the public nature of their faith. The priority of most members was the establishment of a familiar, secure structure in an unfamiliar place. However, Anglican migrants had an appreciation of their church as a public place in which others could meet God and understood that their beliefs and practices were to be shared with others. In answer to the question, 'do they think church expansion through migration is mission?' Anglican migrants in Congo referred to the agency of the divine in whatever they do in God's name and suggested that, providentially, it is.

Conclusion

I have provided a model of intent for intercontinental migrants in Africa that may be used to understand other migrant situations. Creating home, re-ordering home and homelessness indicate that amongst migrants there are different priorities in the demonstration of their faith in a new place. Their intentions vary and so will the results. More research on the connections between intercontinental and cross-continental migration and religious affiliation would be welcome.

However, the sense of the 'public-ness' of a religious home is likely to be carried by migrants beyond the African continent. It will be different from the more private perceptions of home and religion found in the west. The missional implications are clear. A priority to establish new congregations in new places is not necessarily a priority for mission. Nevertheless, a commitment to a public expression of faith ensures that missional elements are present in such new congregations. Conversely in cultures, like Britain, where church and home have become private domains into which strangers are not always welcome, a church established in a new area with an intentionally missional aim may become chiefly concerned with the well-being of its members. Intent affects outcome but unintended cultural expectations also influence the missional nature of a church.

Chapter Eight

Hospitality and 'Hanging Out': Churches' engagement with people seeking asylum in the UK

Susanna Snyder

Asylum seeking is one of the most contentious social and political issues in the UK today. Hostility towards 'asylum seekers'[1] is prevalent, asylum policies have become increasingly restrictive and many looking for refuge instead find themselves living in isolation, poverty and fear. A recent report estimated that two-thirds of asylum claims are ultimately refused and that thousands of asylum seekers are living in destitution in London alone.[2] This chapter explores how churches and Christian groups are stepping in to offer vital support and suggests ways in which this hospitality might be enhanced. I am self-consciously writing from the perspective of an ordained, white, middle class, British woman.[3]

Many churches and Christian organisations are offering asylum seekers support and hospitality. Restore, an ecumenical Christian

---

1   The homogenising term 'asylum seeker' is problematic as people seeking asylum are inevitably diverse and complex individuals. However for convenience, it is used here to refer to people applying for refugee status according to the 1951 UN Convention on Refugees.

2   Amnesty International, *Down and Out in London: The road to destitution for rejected asylum seekers* (London: Amnesty International, 2006). Asylum seekers relate their recent experiences in Caroline Moorhead, *Human Cargo: A Journey Among Refugees* (London: Chatto and Windus, 2005) and *I came here for safety: the reality of detention and destitution for asylum seekers* (Coventry Peace House: Coventry, 2006). This can be downloaded from http://covpeacehouse.org.uk/files/I%20came%20here%20for%20 safety.pdf, accessed 4 June 2007

3   There are dangers in speaking on behalf of asylum seekers and the host community. Bell Hooks warns against 'talking about' others and erasing their voices in *Yearning: race, gender and cultural politics* (Boston: South End Press, 1990), pp. 125-126.

organisation in Birmingham, offers one-to-one volunteer befriending, a summer holiday programme for children and awareness-raising sessions. They also provide information and support for a variety of local church groups, which in turn undertake everything from providing English classes, clothes and food to campaigning against inflammatory media coverage. Across the UK, Christian volunteers accompany asylum seekers to court hearings and MP surgeries, visit people held in removal centres and offer day-to-day practical advice and emotional support.[4] National Christian networks – notably the Churches Refugee Network, Enabling Christians in Serving Refugees and the National Catholic Refugee Forum – have also been set up to support refugees and churches working with them.

Others contribute by engaging in the public debate. In 2005, over forty-five church leaders supported Church Action on Poverty's 'Living Ghosts' campaign against policy-induced destitution among asylum seekers. In 2006, the Commission on Urban Life and Faith challenged the government to take a responsible lead on asylum policy and condemned policies which deny asylum seekers the right to work.[5] Church Action on Poverty, the Church of England and the Catholic Bishops' Conference are currently partners in the national 'Still Human, Still Here' Campaign, co-ordinating sleep-out protests against destitution as well as the lobbying of MPs.[6]

These activities are making a significant contribution to the well-being of asylum seekers. Alice Bloch claims that a refugee's settlement in the UK is affected by four factors – government policies, social networks, the characteristics of individual migrants and their circumstances of migration.[7] Churches are positively involved in trying to improve the first two of these. They are tackling policy through lobbying and campaigning and at the same time, are providing essential social contacts for people outside their immediate ethnic or

---

4   www.ecsr.org.uk lists some church-related projects. This paper focuses on the work of mainstream historic denominations.

5   *Faithful Cities: A call for celebration, vision and justice* (London: Church House, 2006), p. 90.

6   See http://www.church-poverty.org.uk/campaigns/livingghosts/, accessed 4 June 2007.

7   Alice Bloch, *The Migration and Settlement of Refugees in Britain* (Aldershot: Palgrave Macmillan, 2002), p. 80.

asylum-seeking communities. Moreover, churches are often a first port of call for those are seeking help and support, being perceived as safe places, and this is perhaps especially true for those who have been a practising member of a faith community in their country of origin. As Elizabeth Ferris has suggested, NGOs and particularly churches have an important practical and political role to play in supporting refugees. Not only do they have an advantage in being able to listen to the voices of those seeking asylum at a grassroots level, but they also

> possess certain strengths which challenge the hegemony of governments. They control funds and human resources which governments may need. They have access to information which may contradict government sources. They may have constituencies capable of mobilizing public opinion... the Churches stand out from NGOs since they possess not only large numbers of adherents but also a certain moral authority which may be used to sway public opinion.[8]

Furthermore, Christian groups are often plugging glaring gaps in mainstream statutory provision for asylum seekers.[9] *The Boaz Trust* in Manchester is a striking example: it uses four houses and other rooms in volunteer's homes to accommodate those who are 'end-of-process' and destitute.[10] Significantly, in an urban white paper of 2000, *Our Town and Cities: The Future*, the government itself recognised the vital contribution made by faith communities in situations of deprivation –

> Faith communities can command valuable resources and social capital in terms of networks, buildings, voluntary activity and leadership skills. These can be especially important in deprived areas if other forms of institutional support have been eroded.[11]

---

8 E Ferris, 'The Churches, Refugees and Politics' in G Loescher & L Monahan, eds. *Refugees and International Relations* (Oxford: Clarendon Press, 1989), p. 175.

9 Bloch mentions the importance of Refugee Community Organisations, but not churches, in filling gaps in refugee provision. See *Migration and Settlement*, p. 161.

10 See http://www.boaztrust.org.uk/, accessed 4 June 2007.

11 See http://www.communities.gov.uk/index.asp?id=1127168, accessed 4 June 2007. This contribution is however seldom acknowledged by those working in mainstream Migration and Refugee Studies.

The hospitality offered by Christians to asylum seekers is unquestionably important and one of the most impressive characteristics of church groups is that when a problem arises or a need is perceived, people tend to get stuck in immediately. However, this means there is often little time to reflect and ask deeper questions. Are there any drawbacks in the ways we currently offer support? How might our hospitality be improved?

The 'Bigger Picture': Understanding the Dynamics of Forced Migration

One way in which Christians could improve their support of asylum seekers is by understanding more about how the experience of asylum seekers in the UK fits within the national and global political context and is 'shaped by existing socio-economic systems'.[12] This could help us to move beyond a reactive, 'sticking plaster' response to one which also involves addressing the many underlying, complex and interrelated *causes* of asylum seekers' problems.[13]

Do we, for example, realise how complex the reasons for most refugee movements are? While there are different categories of migration recognised in law, including skilled migration, family reunion, economic migration and asylum seeking, Stephen Castles claims that with the globalisation, there has been 'a diversification, proliferation and intermingling' of these in practice over the last twenty years.[14] Most migrants can no longer be fitted into one specific category due to the complex interaction of personal choice and structural causes in their movement. Migrants of all 'types' are motivated both by 'push-factors', aspects of life at home which encourage them to leave, and 'pull-factors', perceived benefits of living in a new country – albeit in different proportions.[15] 'Push' factors include political persecution, environmental disaster and

---

12 Saskia Sassen, *Guests and Aliens* (New York: The New Press, 1999), p. 155.

13 See A R Zolberg & P M Benda, (eds.), *Global Migrants, Global Refugees: Problems and Solutions* (New York: Berghahn Books, 2001).

14 S Castles, 'Migration and Community Formation under Conditions of Globalization', *International Migration Review* Volume 26.4 (Winter 2002), pp1148-1151., p1151. See also Nicholas Van Hear, *New Diasporas* (London: UCL Press, 1998)

15 Kunz discusses 'push' and 'pull' factors in 'The refugees in flight, kinetic models and forms of displacement', *IRM* 7 (1971), pp125-146

degradation, conflict and civil war, rape and poverty. However, the definition still used by the Home Office to determine whether someone should be granted asylum is the 1951 UN Convention on Refugees which requires proof of 'individual political persecution'.[16] Should we therefore be challenging such outdated definitions of 'asylum seeker' and 'refugee' and encouraging greater nuance in legal and political discourse?

Second, do we understand the causal link between our foreign policy and the arrival of asylum seekers? Applications for asylum in the UK from Iraqis increased substantially after the invasion in 2001, and it is clear that external military intervention significantly increases refugee movements.[17]

Third, how often do we recognise the implications which our own economic needs have on asylum seekers? Asylum seekers make a vital contribution to the low-level service sector through doing a vast range of menial jobs. In doing these jobs for wages well below the minimum because they are not permitted to work legally, they act as 'capitalism's lubricant'. Thus our need for 'a cheap and often compliant workforce' encourages policies barring asylum seekers from legal employment. [18] This in turn keeps them in poverty and prevents them from contributing to the official economy, which then ironically becomes one of the sticks used to beat them.

Fourth, do we recognise the complex interplay between public opinion, the media and the government in the creation of asylum policies and the treatment of asylum seekers?[19] Public fear and hostility can influence policy, but asylum seekers can also be very useful political scapegoats when health, education and housing

---

16 The UN Convention of 1951 defines a 'refugee' as someone who, 'owing to a well-founded fear of being persecuted for reasons of race, religion, nationality, membership of a particular group or political opinion, is outside the country of his nationality and is unable or, owing to such fear, is unwilling to avail himself of the protection of that country'.

17 See S Scmeidl, 'Conflict and Forced Migration: A Quantative Review, 1964-1995' in ibid., pp62-94.

18 Marfleet, *Refugees*, pp. 172, 263.

19 See Paul Statham and Shamit Saggar in Sarah Spencer, ed., *The Politics of Migration: Managing Opportunity, Conflict and Change* (Oxford: Blackwell, 2003).

provision seem to be failing. They provide a 'ready target for campaigns which seek enemies'[20] and act as convenient chaotic 'others' in contrast to which a sense of coherent national identity can be formed.

A Root Cause: Challenging the Fear of the 'Stranger'

A second way in which Christians could enhance their hospitality is by engaging with and tackling people's fear of asylum seekers, a significant underlying cause for their difficulties once they have arrived in the UK. Those who perceive immigration as a direct threat to an established way of life and scarce resources worry about diluting British culture and fear increases in crime and competition for jobs and housing.[21] These surface anxieties actually have deep roots. *Faithful Cities*, a recent report by the Commission on Urban Life and Faith, outlines how globalisation has brought with it a growing sense of insecurity due to 'uncertainties of mobile capital, flexible labour markets, declining government legitimacy, the erosion of collective welfare and the transfer of risk to individuals.' Those searching for identity, belonging and certainty in such a mobile and fragile context are likely to guard their territories far more jealously and aggressively against different 'others' who symbolise all that threatens them.[22]

Since 9/11 and the July 2005 terrorist attacks in London, asylum seeking and immigration have been increasingly linked with terrorism and national security.[23] Revisiting Hobbes's observations of life in 17th century England, Jan Huysmans explores our contemporary fear of foreigners. The abstract fear of death is transformed into something tangible by locating it in agents who are different from us and have the power to kill us. Thus 'the fear of the other is an objectified fear of death'.[24] When migrants or asylum seekers become linked with

---

20 Philip Marfleet, *Refugees in a Global Era* (Basingstoke: Palgrave Macmillan, 2006), p. 263.

21 See Stephen Castles, *Ethnicity and Globalization* (London: SAGE, 2000), p. 191.

22 *Faithful Cities*, p. 19.

23 See Matthew J Gibney, 'Security and the ethics of asylum after 11 September', *Forced Migration Review* 13 (2002).

24 Jan Huysmans, 'Migrants as a security problem: dangers of 'securitizing' societal issues' in R Miles and D Thränhardt, *Migration and European Integration* (London: Pinter, 1995), p. 58.

terrorism, they become identified as carriers of death who are negatively and stereotypically defined as undifferentiated 'non-I's. Reasoning as the threatened host, Huysman concludes, 'Migration causes violence, and violence kills...the migrant carries death and who wants to host death?' [25]

Such fear, uncertainty and insecurity are particularly pronounced in urban communities of social deprivation and hardship where asylum seekers are often housed. Manuel Castells refers to 'black holes' in our cities which 'concentrate in their density all the destructive energy that affects humanity from multiple sources.'[26] Ironically, it is precisely those already living in these 'black holes' or ghettos, the urban underclass, who are expected to host others who are marginalized. This only exacerbates feelings of anxiety, fear and anger which can so easily turn into hostility towards anyone perceived to be 'outside' or strange.

There is a danger that some of us engaged with asylum seekers dismiss these fears. We split society into those who are 'good,' generally in favour of granting asylum, and those who are 'bad,' thus against it. We criticise all hostility and concentrate solely on supporting asylum seekers. I am not suggesting that we should not react strongly against ill-informed hostility – this is clearly important and right. What I am suggesting is that we need to develop a more expansive and complex hospitality.

We need to recognise that sometimes, reluctance to share already inadequate public spaces and overstretched public services is natural. Moreover, we need to be wary of demanding an openness and generosity which we ourselves seem unable or unwilling to offer. At present, churches rarely succeed in engaging with the urban underclass or offering them the frontline, daily hospitality which they are required to show asylum seekers. Should we therefore be linking our efforts to support asylum seekers with efforts to tackle the poverty and deprivation experienced by many who are hostile? Should we challenge government policies which place asylum seekers in urban 'black holes'? Should we actively engage with those who are anti-asylum and address their underlying fears? Not only do encounter and

---

25 Huysmans, 'Migrants', p. 60.

26 Manuel Castells, *End of Millennium* (Second Edition, Oxford: Blackwell, 2000), p. 165.

conversation help break down stereotypes and build trust, but as urban planning theorist Leonie Sandercock suggests, flourishing, multicultural communities can only be built by working *through* people's fears and anxieties.[27] Inner city parish churches are perhaps ideally placed to understand, engage with and transform negative attitudes towards the 'stranger': not only are they supposed to have grassroots contact with everyone in the community, but the Christian insight that strangers can be life-bringing could be a powerful resource for countering fear.

The Christian Tradition: Recognising the 'Stranger' as Life-Bringer

This insight that strangers are potential life-bringers and God-bearers is a thread woven through the Old and New Testaments. In the Hebrew Bible, the book of Ruth demonstrates how showing hospitality to strangers can be life-enhancing for the host. When Ruth, a Moabite, arrives in Israel, Boaz cares for and marries her. They then have a son, Obed, who brings new life and joy to all.[28] In the stories of Abraham welcoming three strangers in Mamre (Gen. 18. 1-15) and the widow's generosity towards Elijah (1 Kings 17-18), the generous sharing of food provides the context for divine revelation and new life. [29] The author of Hebrews stresses the need to recognise the gifts brought by guests, stating, 'Do not neglect to show hospitality to strangers, for by doing that some have entertained angels without knowing it' (Heb. 13.2). Jesus' exchanges with Zaccheus (Lk. 19.1-10), the woman in Samaria (Jn. 4.1-42) and the disciples on the Emmaus Road (Lk. 24. 13-35) make clear that all who offer hospitality to Jesus, the ultimate stranger, are never left unchanged.

It is not surprising then that theologians have frequently identified strangers as those who can offer us glimpses of God and thus help us to see in a new way. Martin Buber, famous for articulating the 'I-Thou' principle, suggests that encounters with others can tear 'us away to dangerous extremes, loosening the well-tried context, leaving more

---

27 Leonie Sandercock, *Cosmopolis II: Mongrel Cities* (London: Continuum, 2003), p. 138.

28 See André LaCocque, *Ruth: A Continental Commentary* (trans. K C Hanson; Minneapolis: Fortress, 2004).

29 Clare Amos, *The Book of Genesis* (Peterborough: Epworth, 2004), p. 102.

questions than satisfaction behind them, shattering security...'[30] Being open to others is disturbing and therefore potentially life-changing. More recently, Walter Brueggemann and Miroslav Volf have written about the importance of relating to others for our own sake as well as for theirs. For Brueggemann, 'otherness' in terms of God, neighbour and within our self, is the very source of our being, and we need to learn how to 'other' with courage and grace.[31] Volf uses the active verb 'embrace' to suggest how we should relate to other. Embracing involves welcoming, self-giving and readjusting our own identities to make space for others to enter in.[32] It is through encountering difference in the stranger that we can develop, gain new insights and be transformed:

> Identity is a result of the distinction from the other *and* the internalisation of the relationship to the other...The self is dialogically constructed. The other is already from the outset part of the self. I am who I am in relation to the other.[33]

Christians are called to recognise that in serving our neighbour in practical, concrete ways, their lives may be changed and enriched in the process. As Thomas Ogletree writes,

> To offer hospitality to the stranger is to welcome something new, unfamiliar, and unknown into our life-world. On the one hand, hospitality requires a recognition of the stranger's vulnerability in an alien social world. Strangers need shelter and sustenance in their travels, especially when they are moving through a hostile environment. On the other hand, hospitality designates occasions of potential discovery which can open up our narrow provincial worlds. Strangers have stories to tell which... display the finitude and relativity of our orientation to meaning... The stranger does not simply

---

30 Martin Buber, *I and Thou* (Edinburgh: T & T Clark, 1937), p. 34.

31 Walter Brueggemann, *The Covenanted Self: Explorations in Law and Covenant* (Minneapolis: Fortress Press, 1999), pp. 16-17.

32 Miroslav Volf, *Exclusion and Embrace: A Theological Exploration of Identity, Otherness and Reconciliation* (Nashville: Abingdon Press, 1996), p. 29.

33 Volf, *Exclusion*, pp. 66, 91.

challenge or subvert our assumed world of meaning; she may enrich, even transform, that world.[34]

Or as Christine Pohl puts it: 'In joining physical, spiritual and social nourishment, hospitality is a life-giving practice. It is both fruitful and fertile.'[35] According to Henri Nouwen, the notion that 'fearful strangers can become guests' and that 'in the context of hospitality, guest and host can reveal their most precious gifts and bring new life to each other' is an intrinsically Biblical one.[36]

This theological and biblical principle is echoed by many who currently work or volunteer with asylum seekers: they speak of receiving much from those they are assisting. Some mention asylum seekers' generous hospitality, their contributions to our cultural life and the joy of sharing in the birth of a baby or a child's successful first day at school. The sense of community within some support groups gives volunteers a place to belong as much as it does asylum seekers. I have been astounded, challenged and touched by the trust in God and offers of friendship I have encountered. While such examples may sound trite, the ways in which we are enriched go much deeper through subconscious or gentle shifts in our understanding and perspective.

However, it is also important to acknowledge that strangers have not always been so well regarded in the Christian tradition. In the Hebrew Bible, foreigners are frequently seen as people to be destroyed or at the very least, avoided.[37] Nations including Egypt, Babylon and Assyria are regarded as absolute enemies and God promises to annihilate 'the Amorites, the Hittites, the Perizzites, the Canaanites, the Hivites and the Jebusites'.[38] In Ezra 9-10 and Nehemiah 13.23-31,

---

34 Thomas Ogletree, *Hospitality to the Stranger: Dimensions of Moral Understanding* (Philadelphia: Fortress Press, 1985), pp. 2-3.

35 Christine Pohl, *Making Room: Recovering Hospitality as a Christian Tradition* (Grand Rapids, Michigan: Eerdmans, 1999), p. 13.

36 Henri Nouwen, *Reaching Out* (Glasgow: Collins, 1976), pp. 63-65. It is important though to acknowledge that encounters with strangers do not always enrich us or bring new life.

37 Daniel L Smith-Christopher, 'Between Ezra and Isaiah: Exclusion, Transformation and Inclusion of the "Foreigner" in Post-Exilic Biblical Theology' in Mark Brett, (ed.), *Ethnicity and the Bible* (Leiden: Brill, 1996), p. 117-142.

38 Exod. 23.23.

social contact between Israelites and foreigners is forbidden and mixed marriages condemned. At the end of the book of Esther, we learn that 'the Jews struck down all their enemies with the sword, slaughtering, and destroying them, and did as they pleased to those who hated them.'[39] These are a few of the texts which Smith-Christopher recognises 'could be used to justify racist and oppressive attitudes and policies towards anyone considered the "foreigner" or "enemy".'[40] Christians need to counter passages and stories which could be used to justify any oppression of asylum seekers.[41]

'Hanging Out' rather than being 'Monsters of Concern'

As well as drawing on the insight that strangers can be 'life-bringers' to counter host population fear, it is also important for Christians to recognise the implications of this for their own work. This is the final way in which I would like to suggest that we could improve our hospitality. One danger of caring for asylum seekers is that we can view the link between church supporters and asylum seekers as one-way traffic: 'we' are the people who support or serve 'them'. 'We' are actively doing good and 'they' are passively receiving. Clearly, if strangers are God bearers, this paternalistic perception is inaccurate. However, it is still common and can have a very negative impact on asylum seekers.

Barbara Harrell-Bond has challenged the ways in which NGOs and humanitarian agencies offer aid. She questions Western notions of compassion which are often 'inherently ethnocentric, paternalistic and non-professional' and emphasises the need for refugee participation.[42] Criticizing the 'myopia of outsiders', she claims that we need to scrutinize our work, acting as facilitators rather than imposers of aid and being accountable to those whom we wish to help.[43] She warns of

---

39 Est. 9.5.

40 Smith-Christopher, 'Between Ezra', p. 118. Julia Kristeva maintains that in the Middle Ages, monasteries and churches only offered hospitality to those who were Christian. See *Strangers to Ourselves* (New York: Columbia University Press, 1991), pp. 86-87.

41 See R S Sugirtharajah, *Postcolonial Reconfigurations: An Alternative Way of Reading the Bible and Doing Theology* (London: SCM, 2003), p. 2.

42 Barbara Harrell-Bond, *Imposing Aid* (New York: OUP, 1986), 26.

43 Harrell-Bond, *Imposing*, 335, 366.

the dangers of being 'monsters of concern'. [44] The ways in which refugees are 'helped' can be a debilitating source of stress, as refugees are required to be grateful, placed in the role of helpless children and are frequently patronized. In the 1950s, Hungarian refugees in the USA were often expected by their church sponsors to conform, but without having it explained how they were to do so. She writes, 'Refugees attract 'volunteers'... who often behave as though they 'need refugees more than refugees need them'. As Michael Ignatieff astutely points out, fulfilling people's *needs* is very different from helping strangers to *flourish*, something which involves the intangible qualities of love and belonging, dignity, respect and ultimate meaning. [45]

Could we therefore perhaps re-imagine our work with asylum seekers as 'hanging out'? Graeme Rodgers describes 'hanging out' as having 'informal, interpersonal and 'everyday' types of encounters' which allows the space for forced migrant voices to be heard. [46] 'Hanging out' like this, without a pre-set agenda, could and does help asylum seekers to participate and speak on their own terms. A listening ear, respect, friendship, informal chat and laughter are some of the valuable gifts that many Christians already offer. This kind of 'hanging out' together could also create room for asylum seekers' very different gifts to be brought and recognised. This is not to suggest that Christians should not be 'professional' experts, but only that any expertise we do have always needs to be offered sensitively and in partnership with those we seek to support. [47]

---

44 Harrell-Bond, *Imposing*, p363. Quoting John O'Neill, Making Sense Together: *an introduction to wild sociology* (1975), p64

45 Michael Ignatieff, *The Needs of Strangers* (New York: Picador, 1984), p. 15. Barbara Harrell-Bond suggests that the ways in which refugees are 'helped' can be a debilitating source of stress. See 'The experience of refugees as recipients of aid' in Alastair Ager, (ed.), *Refugees: Perspectives on the Experience of Forced Migration* (London: Continuum, 1999), pp. 136-168.

46 Graeme Rodgers, ''Hanging out' with forced migrants: methodological and ethical challenges', *Forced Migration Review* 21 (September 2004), 48.

47 On the importance of professional expertise, see Susan Forbes Martin, 'Forced Migration and Professionalism', *International Review of Migration* Volume 35.1 (Spring 2001), pp226-243.

Changing Christian thinking

Chapter Nine

Exile, seeking asylum in the UK and the *Missio Dei*

Nicholas Sagovsky

I have not myself had the experience of exile. I have, however, spent a great deal of time with people who are exiles – almost always in this country - and my father's family were exiled from their native Russia when he was a child. I have no doubt that this caesura in their lives, when the society they had known was completely destroyed by revolution and civil war, left a profound imprint on the whole family.

For some peoples – the Jews, the Palestinians, the Chagos Islanders – the experience of exile has been determinative of their identity. Others – notably indigenous people – have become exiles in their own lands, alienated, sometimes with a genocidal ferocity, from ways of life that have sustained their culture for generations. For some nomadic peoples, such as the Maasai or the herdsman of Darfur, their sense of 'home' differs from that of settled, agricultural peoples. Nevertheless, pressures of encroaching urbanisation and of changing climate, together with deliberate political pressures, may cause them to be exiled from lands that have sustained their traditional way of life for generations. We think of exile as enforced absence from home-land; it may just as much be enforced alienation from a traditional way of making a home.

I have been asked to reflect, from a biblical and missiological perspective, on the experience of exile, migration and dispossession. Simply, however, to seek to understand would be, in Marx's terms, to be a philosopher ('The philosophers have only interpreted the world in various ways; the point is, to change it.') I take it that a missiological perspective is one which seeks to understand situations in the light of the *Missio Dei* and that the *Missio Dei* is always transformative of the human situation. I shall be concerned, then, to ask what kind of initiatives can and should be taken in the light of the *Missio Dei* to transform the experience of those who have come to the UK as exiles. Most of what I have to say will focus on one particular group: those who have come as asylum seekers. This is because my first-hand experience is very largely of this group, particularly of those who have been refused asylum.[1] However the experience of exile is of course much broader than that.

If we ask why people become exiles, we need to make a few distinctions. First of all, there is the distinction between those who are *voluntary exiles* and those who are involuntary exiles. This is only a rough distinction because for many who opt to leave their home and move somewhere else, there are pressures which make it a far from free choice. Hunger or a lack of job opportunities may cause a person to move and that person may well experience this as 'being exiled' rather than as voluntary migration. In the nineteenth century, many Irish people migrated to America because there were better economic opportunities there – but when the potato harvest failed they migrated because if they stayed in Ireland they and their families would starve. And then there were Irish and Scots who were driven out by clearances: they were forcibly and violently exiled from their land.

To talk of 'economic migration' as voluntary migration is over simple. It is also over simple to see economic migration as permanent migration. Many economic migrants, such as Philippinos or Poles working in Britain, have strong family ties at home and their remittances are a vital part of the wider family budget. With the ease of modern travel, they work abroad almost as one might work in another town of one's native land. However, they may not be fluent in English, they will not be familiar with English culture and customs, and it will take time before they feel in any sense 'at home' in a

---

1   What I say later about the experience of asylum-seekers applies both to those who are refused but not returned and to those whose cases drag on for years. The difficulties of exile are experienced also by those whose claims are accepted and who then have to face fresh challenges of integration.

foreign land. For some it will be important that they see themselves as temporary migrants who can anticipate return to their country of origin. Others may intend to settle in Britain, or gradually become settled in Britain to the point where they marry and buy property. Integration and assimilation is one route to the ending of exile.

Some people are much more clearly *involuntary exiles*. The key difference is that the voluntary exile is free to go back home, the involuntary exile is not. This may be because 'home' is temporarily or permanently uninhabitable, whether through natural disaster such as an earthquake, or human intervention, such as a war. Where there is a large-scale disaster, whether famine or fighting, or even the rumour of such a disaster, it may be that a whole population becomes exiled. Sometimes, as in the Soviet Union under Stalin, whole peoples are deliberately and forcibly displaced. Sometimes, as with the anti-semitic policies of Hitler, the persecution and displacement applies only to one group within society. As the situation worsened towards Hitler's 'Final Solution', the choice that faced European Jews was stark: exile or death. There is, of course, one other form of involuntary exile that has today almost become a matter of history: exile as punishment. It is, however, important to remember the punitive connotations of exile for Ovid or for Napoleon – and, within a Deuteronomic framework, of the Jews in Babylon. We might see this as a 'limit' situation, which reminds us of the way exile has been used to subdue and punish individuals and populations. We should not be surprised at the depth of suffering involved.

Most exiles today have taken an initiative to flee their homeland. What all such exiles have in common is that in some respect they, or their families, have chosen or been forced to seek a better life. Almost always, this has been, and it may well continue to be, a traumatic and risky undertaken. Exile may be to terrible conditions in a refugee camp, but at least with the hope of escaping death and of return to the home country. For those seeking refuge, their exile may well be accompanied by fear of capture, privation, separation from friends, family or community, difficulties of travel, the fear of rejection, pervasive uncertainty about the future. But also, in all these circumstances, there is hope of living, whether temporarily or permanently, in a better place. In the story of the exile from Eden (which, it should be noted, is seen as punitive in Gen 3:16-24) the

143

phenomenon of exile is taken as a metaphor for the human condition; the hope that exiles carry of 'a better country' is seen in the Epistle to the Hebrews (cf. 11:14-16) as a metaphor for the life of faith. The most destructive thing that can happen to an exile is the loss of hope; the most constructive, settlement in a secure 'home'.

A Human Rights Approach

In speaking about the experience of those who have sought asylum in Britain, I need to make a couple of initial remarks. The first is that, according to International Law, people in need of protection have a right to expect such protection within their own state and, if they leave their own state because they do not receive the protection they need, to seek it in another state. This is the nub of refugee law: when a person applies for such protection in a foreign country, he or she is asking to be recognised as a refugee. According to the Refugee Convention (1951), if they are acknowledged to have a 'well-founded fear of persecution based on their race, religion, nationality, or membership of a political or social group' then they should receive refugee status in the country where they have applied for it, or in another country to which they may, with their assent, be moved.[2]

There are some serious problems about this definition, which was framed after the Second World War, when the experience of Jews, who had been in desperate need of protection but had been turned away from countries like the UK, was painfully recent. At the time of the formation of the United Nations and the drafting of the Universal Declaration of Human Rights, this was what was uppermost in people's minds. Only after 1967 was there added to the Refugee Convention a Protocol which made it applicable in similar situations worldwide. However, no thought was given to the sheer scale of the need for protection that might occur, nor to the ease with which people might travel round the globe to seek that protection. The terms of the Refugee Convention are relatively tightly drawn: to receive protection a person has to demonstrate that they have a *well-founded* fear of persecution. Fear in itself is not an adequate trigger (however much

---

2   One magisterial text from amongst many on this subject is James Hathaway's *The Rights of Refugees under International Law* (Cambridge: Cambridge University Press, 2005). See also, Matthew J. Gibney, *The Ethics and Politics of Asylum* (Cambridge: Cambridge University Press, 2004), especially pp.1-22.

one understands and sympathises with the fears of people who have been through terrible and traumatic experiences). More than that, it has to be fear of persecution – that is to say state-orchestrated intimidation or violence, or at least a refusal on the part of police and state authorities to protect particular target groups or individuals.

What is now recognised in the UK, and particularly after the incorporation of the European Convention of Human Rights into UK law in 1998, is that though a person may not qualify for refugee status, it may be a breach of their human rights to send them back to their country of origin. In cases, for instance, where, simply because someone has tried to claim asylum in the UK, they are in danger of cruel or inhuman treatment in their country of origin, sending them back may be seen as a breach of their human rights. The same might be true if just one member of a family were being sent back (against the right to family life) or a person who has a potentially fatal medical condition such as AIDS is to be sent back to a country where the appropriate treatment is not available (so that their right to life is imperilled). We should also note, in passing, that there are certain countries to which it is practically impossible to return people, either because the country itself is a war zone, or because the authorities refuse to provide documentation for returns.

The approach to asylum claims in the UK is thus governed by an understanding which is framed in terms of human rights. In this there is a missiological challenge. Some Christians have been extremely dubious about human rights thinking, believing it to lack an adequate basis in Biblical and Christian tradition.[3] In response to that, we have indeed to grant that the formation of the concept of human rights as we have it today was much indebted to secular thinkers like Tom Paine and Thomas Jefferson who saw in 'natural rights' and the 'rights of man' a counterweight to the authority of the Church, which was so quick to stress human duties. Nevertheless there is a strand of Christian thinking about the 'right' and about 'natural rights' which can be traced from a text like Proverbs 31:8 (NRSV): 'Speak out for those who cannot speak, for the rights of all the destitute,' through

---

3   This is discussed in Esther D. Reed, *The Ethics of Human Rights* (Waco, Texas: Baylor University Press, 2007), especially pp. 1-42.

Aquinas,[4] to the contributions made by liberal Protestants to the Universal Declaration of Human Rights.[5]

The discussion about the relation between Christianity and human rights continues today, even though the Roman Catholic and Anglican Churches have now very much taken human rights into their thinking and practice, especially since Vatican 2. There is simply no other publicly accepted and understood discourse in which to speak about the needs of the poor, the destitute and the marginalised, in such a way that the meeting of those needs becomes justiceable. The socialist suspicion of human rights and preference for thinking in terms of human solidarity has been shown to be much less effective and much more open to abuse than human rights thinking, which, though itself open to abuse - for instance by the invention of 'rights' that favour the rich and powerful - is constantly open to critical public correction. There are other forms of discourse available to discuss human flourishing, such as that of 'capabilities' popularised by Sen and Nussbaum, but they are harder to deploy in terms of law.[6] At its root, the term 'human right' is not so far from 'the right' as it is spoken of in the Bible, and the struggle for human rights is not so far from the struggle for righteousness or right relations. Christians may not (and should not) be entirely comfortable with human rights discourse and practice, but there is nothing else that can prove as effective in the public domain.

Having said that, for a Christian the language of human rights needs to be supplemented with the language of hospitality. Again and again the Scriptures teach hospitality towards strangers. For people who are exiled, such hospitality becomes of vital importance. It is likely that a Christian individual or a church will think in terms of offering hospitality to strangers than in terms of defending their human rights. This may help to account for the prominence of people of faith in a whole range of welcome organisations, but the relative ineffectuality of

---

4   See Roger Ruston, *Human Rights and the Image of God* (London: SCM, 2004), pp. 40-57.

5   See John Nurser, *For All Peoples and Nations, Christian Churches and Human Rights* (Geneva: WCC Publications, 2005).

6   For an overview, see Martha C. Nussbaum, *Women and Human Development, the Capabilities Approach* (Cambridge: Cambridge University Press, 2000), pp. 4-15.

faith organisations in resisting or challenging ever more draconian immigration legislation.

If Christians have been relatively ineffectual in defending the human rights of exiles in the UK, Christians have participated very fully in overseas development. In the second part of this paper I shall be concentrating on the relatively small group of migrants who seek asylum in the UK.[7] A very much larger number of migrants seek asylum in countries neighbouring those where there are civil upheavals or natural disasters: the presence of refugees within a society is largely a phenomenon of the developing world, which places huge burdens on relatively weak or undeveloped economies. The aid that is given to such countries to support and eventually to assist the return of such refugees is a major part of the strategy of the rich nations to address the refugee problem worldwide. Even more significant than aid efforts, however, is the development of trade. Fair trade organisations point prophetically towards terms of trade which can help to keep people on their land and give them an investment in a stable infrastructure. In this way, 'rights' to education, health care and to good work are addressed and promoted.

This brings us closer to naming the real drivers of migration in the contemporary world. Here we can only allude to the impact of global warming, but its importance for future migration and exile is immense. One of the main drivers of migration is, of course, natural disaster – and the political aspect to the *impact* of natural disaster should not be overlooked. The impact of hurricane Katrina fell disproportionately on the poor of New Orleans, driving them from their homes. Amartya Sen has long argued that true democracies do not experience famines – and we know that the impact of famines falls disproportionately on the poor.[8] There is an overlap between the phenomena of natural disaster and the lack of human rights. There is also the underlying problem of absolute poverty: poverty of resources to resist the impact of flood, drought and deprivation of human rights – but another key problem is that of global inequality. R.G. Wilkinson has done magnificent work

---

7 The distinction between migrants in general and asylum seekers in particular is fundamental to Paul Weller ed., *Migration Principles, Statement for Churches Working on Migration Issues* (London: CTBI and CCRJ, 2007) .

8 See 'Famine and Other Crises' in Amartya Sen, *Development as Freedom* (Oxford: Oxford University Press, 1999), pp. 160-88.

which shows that human beings can cope with extraordinary levels of deprivation if they do not experience this as inequality.[9] What exacerbates ill-health, shortens lives, and brings about failure to flourish is perceived levels of inequality. The more inequality there is within or between societies the higher will be the level of social pathology. This is of enormous importance both internationally – where the levels of wealth and opportunity between nations vary so hugely – and within a nation. Exiles caught within the UK asylum system have their unequal status rubbed in by their stigmatisation (I use the metaphor deliberately) as indigents in a land of plenty.

At every stage the UK asylum system reinforces the pain and deprivation of exile. I now want to look at this in more detail, as a study of this extreme and liminal situation can illuminate wider features of the experience of exile and show how it can be confronted within the *Missio Dei*.

I shall be talking in terms of experience, and must emphasis once more that all I can do is empathise.[10] This has not been my experience, and I guess that the experience is literally unimaginable to those who have not been through it themselves. I can simply assemble the fragments as they have been communicated to me – much as I can assemble fragments of human experience by listening to the longing and extraordinary bitterness which reflects the experience of exile in Psalm 137, linking that with the longing and bitterness in the experience of exiles today.

The experience of flight and application for asylum

People arrive in Britain and claim asylum by many different routes and for many different reasons. In recent years, the numbers applying have dropped dramatically as it has become ever more difficult to

---

9   R.G. Wilkinson, *Unhealthy Societies, the Afflictions of Inequality* (London: Routledge, 1996).

10 I shall later in this paper refer to the work of the Independent Asylum Commission, which has assembled a great deal of evidence about the experience of people within the UK asylum system. Testimonies from seven public hearings, as well as other testimonies given by individuals, can be viewed on the websites of the Independent Asylum Commission (http://www.independentasylumcommission.org.uk/) and on Human Rights TV (http://www.takethepebble.com/humanrightstv/).

reach these shores. In 2002 the number applying for asylum was 84,000; in 2006 it was 24,000. This is not because the world has become a safer or less troubled place. Some conflicts have abated; others have got worse. Currently, the main countries producing asylum seekers are Eritrea, Afghanistan, Iran, China and Somalia.[11]

Simply to name these countries is to suggest that those who have managed to reach Britain are likely to have come through difficult situations in their own country and to have risked a great deal in making their escape. They are also likely to have experienced difficulties and hardships on their journey. As it has become harder to obtain a visa so the premium on trafficking has increased. Traffickers will not only charge enormous sums of money to convey their clients, but will use intimidation of families to make sure that, whatever the outcome of the journey, they receive payment. Many exiles will have come to Britain in expectation of 'fair play' and a welcome. A number of those who arrive to claim asylum will speak no English and have no idea where they are.

The experience of being criminalised

It has now become a criminal offence to travel without proper documentation. As carriers who take passengers without proper documentation are liable to be fined, the carriers themselves are expected to police this. Those who flee persecution may well have to travel with forged or stolen documents. If they are caught, they are treated as criminals. On arrival in Britain they will be prosecuted and the norm will be for them to serve a sentence in a British prison. They will then be transferred to a Removal Centre run by a private company and deported. Through their attempt at flight they have been criminalised, both in the eyes of the UK government and in the eyes of the authorities of the country to which they are returned. We know little about what happens to such persons on their return.

The experience of being disbelieved and unable to prove the truth of what they say

---

11 Information from Home Office statistics (21.8.07): http://www.homeoffice.gov.uk/rds/pdfs07/hosb1407.pdf (accessed 17.12.07).

There are those who flee persecution and turmoil who can plan their escape and take with them essential documents. They are fortunate if they are able to think through and assemble the documents they will need prove their identity and their story. They are doubly fortunate if they anticipate the levels of disbelief they will encounter from the UK Border and Immigration Agency and in the immigration courts and plan accordingly. For many, of course, such planning is impossible. They leave in haste, taking with them whatever they can grab, or simply not returning home after being warned not to do so. Those who have spent time with refused asylum seekers will know how often they struggle to come to terms with the levels of disbelief they encounter when making their claim, and their inability to counter that disbelief with appropriate evidence.

The experience of being disbelieved may well be encountered at the point where an asylum seeker makes their initial claim, is given a substantive interview, and then receives a written decision on their case. Refusal of their claim will often be based on what an immigration official finds credible and incredible. After that (if they are 'fast-tracked,' within days, otherwise within weeks or a few months) the onus is on them to challenge that disbelief in an appeal hearing. They enter the hearing already knowing they have been disbelieved, and they have to intuit the presentation and demeanour that will make them appear believable. In essence, the issue is one of trust: the asylum seeker has entrusted him/herself to the British system only to find they have to stand before a British court bearing the weight of the system's fundamental distrust – something they may feel powerless to refute.

There are those who bear the physical or mental scars of torture, but find that little credence is given to given to them as evidence in the immigration court. This may be because they themselves cannot speak of these things (as often with sexual violence), or because their account of the trauma is not accepted (as with torture that leaves few physical scars), or because their lawyer does not present the material to the court (because medical reports are expensive, take time to prepare and *prove* relatively little), or because the judge discounts them. All of this can be enormously painful and difficult to accept.

The experience of powerlessness and marginalisation

For many who apply for asylum the experience is one of total and paralysing powerlessness. They are claiming a benefit to which they have a human right, but one to which they are more or less powerless to prove their entitlement. The only way in which they can be empowered within the system is by having a competent legal representative. Only a tiny minority of asylum seekers can pay for such representation. Most have to rely on the provision afforded by legal aid – which is strictly limited. They have very little power to compel a lawyer to do effective and timely work. Where lawyers fail them they have very few sanctions.

There are many other ways in which those who have entrusted themselves to the asylum system experience a radical and extensive powerlessness. This applies particularly to those who do not speak English. Simply to understand what is going on may well be virtually impossible. Communication through interpreters can be fraught with difficulty. The first step towards empowerment for many asylum seekers is the learning of English. Attending English classes fulfils a number of purposes but the first must be that of empowerment within an alien culture.

Further experiences of powerlessness often arise from issues to do with the provision of accommodation and subsistence. Asylum seekers are first of all housed in temporary accommodation and then dispersed to accommodation where ever it becomes available. Only in exceptional cases can they express a preference. Some, but by no means all, of the accommodation is excellent – but it will probably be in a completely new area of the country, and may well lead to difficulties of communication with a lawyer, or the need for a change of lawyer. Some accommodation, for instance for disabled persons, is inappropriate; some is run-down. The asylum seeker is relatively powerless to change the situation.

Perhaps the major reason for the experience of powerlessness is the inability to work. For as long as a person does not have refugee status – a period which may last for years – the person cannot legally support themselves through work. With the prohibition on work goes economic and social marginalisation, vulnerability and depression. For some there is also the guilt of having left colleagues and family behind, or being a survivor where others have not survived. All of this contributes to the sense of being cast into limbo and the bitterness of exile.

There is one group for whom the situation is still worse: those who have been refused asylum but cannot be returned to their country of origin. This may be because there is no way physically to return them to a war zone, or it may be because the country refuses them documentation. If they sign an agreement to the effect that they will comply with removal whenever it becomes possible, they are accommodated and given vouchers for necessities, and there they wait. This is asylum 'on the cheap' with total powerlessness to change the situation. These people are without work, without cash, and vulnerable at any time to being moved or removed. Still more vulnerable are those who do not receive or do not accept such provision. They are left destitute, reliant on others for accommodation and food. Needless to say, this renders women especially vulnerable to sexual exploitation.

The experience of being scapegoated and being without voice

One aspect of the situation of the asylum seeker that is especially difficult to bear is the scapegoating that has been exacerbated by the hostility of some sections of the media.[12] The asylum system operates in such a way that the asylum seeker is isolated from mainstream society and rendered indigent from the moment of application. It is not surprising that the 'other' who is powerless to resist is often viewed with suspicion and hostility. In some sections of the media, such as *The Daily Mail*, 'asylum seekers' have frequently been blamed for the very indigence which is forced upon them. For a Christian, who speaks of Jesus 'bearing' the sins of others, the idea that within society certain individuals should be made to bear the anxieties, fears and pain of others, cannot be strange. Just as Jesus was silent before his accusers, so many asylum seekers are without voice to speak of their experience and their predicament. They have entrusted themselves to the receiving community and for some this has led to experiences of marginalisation, rejection and silencing; to an extraordinarily comprehensive loss of human dignity.

---

12 On 'scapegoating', see the fertile discussion in R. Girard, *The Scapegoat* (Baltimore: Johns Hopkins University Press, 1986). This is a fascinating text to read with the experience of people who have sought asylum in mind.

The experience of being without a sustaining community (loss of hope)

One of the striking features of the world of the exile is the importance of the communities that have sprung up to give each other mutual support. This is why exiles from various countries congregate in similar areas of major cities, and then are supported by shops that sell the right sort of ethnic food, by churches, mosques temples and community associations. In a foreign land, the bonds of language and culture, and alienation from the host community, are all the stronger. For older people especially, these support systems are literally life-giving. As we have seen, though, for some of those in the asylum system with long-running cases or cases that have run into the ground, it is simply not possible to opt to be part of such a community. Cheap communication by mobile phone and the internet keeps people in touch, but among exiles loneliness is endemic. For exiles, there is always the dilemma between cultural isolation and integration with the host community. Integration often comes through children and their schooling; for the older generations it is far harder to break barriers down. Those who have come as adults are likely always to feel themselves in a foreign land – and it may well be that the land from which they have come, and which exists in their memory, has gone forever.

How are we to interpret and confront these experiences?

At one level the missiological response to the experience of exiles, and especially of asylum seekers, is obvious. It is a challenge to hospitality – a virtue which is prized in all three Abrahamic faiths. As the author of the Epistle to the Hebrews says, 'Do not neglect to show hospitality, for thereby some have entertained angels unawares' (Hebrews 13:2).[13] There is another level at which it is helpful to reflect on these experiences as experiences of Sheol. Amongst those who have sought asylum are those for whom the whole experience has been one of being trapped in Sheol, the twilight land in which one neither lives nor dies. For me, it was summed up in the experience of

---

13 The NRSV translation of the next verse is, in the context of our argument, suggestive: 'Remember those who are in prison, as though you were in prison with them; those who are being tortured, as though you yourselves were being tortured.' Experience would suggest that is impossible to enter into the *Missio Dei* in this area without being oneself touched by the experience of Sheol.

one friend who had come through what was in effect a concentration camp in Bosnia: 'I am dead', he said, 'but I have to live on for the sake of my children.'

There must be a sense in which the *Missio Dei* is to those who walk 'through the valley of the shadow of death' (Ps 23:4). In the language of Psalm 18:

> The cords of death encompassed me;
> the torrents of perdition assailed me;
> The cords of Sheol entangled me;
> The snares of death confronted me.
>
> (Ps 18:4-5; cf. Ps 116:3)

In both Psalm 18 and Psalm 116, this experience is seen in the context of the Lord's salvation; so also in Psalm 139, where the Psalmist affirms 'If I make my bed in Sheol, you are there' (v. 8). In Jonah, this salvation is embedded within the narrative of the Sheol experience:

> 'I called to the LORD out of my distress,
> and he answered me;
> out of the belly of Sheol I cried,
> and you heard my voice.
> You cast me into the deep,
> into the heart of the seas,
> and the flood surrounded me;
> all your waves and your billows
> passed over me.
> Then I said, "I am driven away
> from your sight;
> how shall I look again
> upon your holy temple?"
> The waters closed in over me;
> the deep surrounded me;
> weeds were wrapped around my head
> at the roots of the mountains.
> I went down to the land
> whose bars closed upon me for ever;
> yet you brought up my life from the Pit,
> O LORD my God. (Jonah 2: 2-6)

Jonah talks about an experience of drowning; many people seeking asylum feel they are 'drowning', asphyxiating, dying within the system.[14]

Another way to speak of this would be to use the language of imprisonment. Some are literally imprisoned in detention centres, and for some of these the experience has a terrible resonance with the abuse they have experienced previously in prisons elsewhere. If the essence of imprisonment is loss of freedom, then the whole asylum system is a form of imprisonment. In this context it is relevant to quote from 1 Peter 3 as one way of expressing the *Missio Dei*:

> For Christ also suffered for sins once for all, the righteous for the unrighteous, in order to bring you to God. He was put to death in the flesh, but made alive in the spirit, in which also he went and made a proclamation to the spirits in prison, who in former times did not obey, when God waited patiently in the days of Noah, during the building of the ark, in which a few, that is, eight people, were saved through water.
>
> (1 Peter 3:18-20)

In its context, the passage addresses the question, 'What happened after Jesus died?' – a question which is answered in terms of the cosmic victory of Christ: he went to preach to the 'spirits in prison who in former times did not obey'. On this was built through the Middle Ages an elaborate mythology of the Harrowing of Hell and of release from Purgatory. Without in any sense wanting to suggest that the suffering of those seeking asylum is punitive, I do want to allude to the motif of the Harrowing of Hell as one way of expressing the *Missio Dei* towards those whose human experience is that of living in a twilight world in which it is impossible to be fully alive as a human being.

The cosmic dimension of the victory of Christ is expressed elsewhere in the New Testament in similar language of universal import: 'so that at the name of Jesus every knee should bend, in heaven and on earth and under the earth, and every tongue confess that Jesus Christ is Lord, to the glory of God the Father' (Phil 2: 10-11). In

---

14 Compare the similar language used of the experience of Hezekiah (Is 38:9-19), and in Psalm 6:4-10 both of which speak powerfully of Sheol, sleeplessness and tears. Again, such experiences are endemic amongst those trapped within the asylum system.

Paul's quasi-narrative account of the *Missio Dei*, it is precisely because Christ 'emptied himself and took the form of a slave' (thus abrogating his freedom) and 'became obedient to the point of death – even death on a cross' that he came directly into touch with the experience of Sheol ('My God, my God, why hast thou forsaken me?'). So low did he sink that his victory has cosmic dimensions. In this narrative it is Jesus himself who is in effect cast into Sheol; in the narrative of the Harrowing of Hell it is Jesus who triumphantly liberates from Sheol.

These experiences can be comprehended within an understanding of the *Missio Dei*, as I have tried to sketch. What makes the link is the hell-ish nature of some human experience. For Christians, who go through this experience, there may be times of finding the presence of Christ vivid and supportive; there may well, as with all those locked into this situation, be times of darkness, of exhaustion, of depression, of the loss of hope and of spiritual disorientation. Any account of the *Missio Dei* must give due weight to these extreme human experiences. What must also be comprehended within such an account is an approach to the structures, *to the system* which is itself the cause of so much suffering, as it holds people in situations of powerlessness and uncertainty despite the fact that all this is remediable by human action. In our fallen world, the social and political structures that are intended to be liberative (in this case to ensure protection for those who need protection) themselves all too easily become instruments of oppression. The goal is freedom: 'For freedom Christ has set us free' (Gal 5:1); or, in terms that reflect and invert the language of Sheol, the goal is life: 'I came that they may have life, and have it abundantly' (Jn 10:10).

Clearly there has to be an asylum system. Claims to asylum must be rigorously tested against refugee law. This will take time – time during which the applicant is bound to experience awful anxiety. Their situation is literally 'liminal'. Some applicants will be refused and there must be a system of returns. Most of those returned will be both disappointed and some will be fearful. There will always be difficult decisions to make. All of this is intrinsic to the politics of living in a fallen world. But the *Missio Dei* is to a fallen world. The Gospel speaks not only to humans oppressed and victimised by human structures, but to those structures themselves.

We are faced with the challenge of the transformative *Missio Dei* and its relevance for the transformation of oppressive social structures. It is this that forms the theological backdrop to my own participation in the Independent Asylum Commission which is currently reviewing the UK Asylum System[15] with the aim of making practical and effective recommendations for change. The Commission will report to the Citizen Organising Foundation, which commissioned this work, in mid-2008. This is an enterprise in the public domain, in which as a Christian, I am working with colleagues of differing faith-commitments. For myself, I see our attempt to review the system and to make recommendations for improvement as entirely within the *Missio Dei*.

'How shall we sing the Lord's sing in a foreign land? (Psalm 137:4). In answer to that question, we have, surely, to look to the hope – despite terrible moments of the experience of Sheol in exile and crucifixion - that pervades the experience of Israel and of the Christian Church:

> I waited patiently for the LORD;
>   he inclined to me and heard my cry.
> He drew me up from the desolate pit,
>   out of the miry bog,
> and set my feet upon a rock,
>   making my steps secure.
> He put a new song in my mouth,
>   a song of praise to our God.
> Many will see and fear,
>   and put their trust in the LORD.
>
>   (Ps 40:1-3)

---

15 See note 9.

Chapter Ten

Strangers in our midst: Mission and migration

Tim Gorringe

Migration

I want to begin with one of history's grumpy old men, the monk Gildas, writing about 540. Gildas, an enthusiast for Roman rule, came from Strathclyde but lived in Wales. The British isles, he says, 'stiff with cold and frost, and in a distant region of the world, remote from the visible sun, received the beams of light, that is, the holy precepts of Christ, the true Sun... at the latter part, as we know, of the reign of Tiberius Caesar, by whom his religion was propagated without impediment, and death threatened to those who interfered with its professors. These rays of light were received with lukewarm minds by the inhabitants, but they nevertheless took root among some of them in a greater or less degree, until nine years' persecution of the tyrant Diocletian.' Unfortunately, as things now stood, the Romans were forced to leave to look after their homeland. As they retreated 'the Picts and Scots, like worms which in the heat of mid-day come forth from their holes, hastily land again from their canoes, in which they had been carried beyond the Cichican valley, differing one from another in manners, but inspired with the same avidity for blood, and all more eager to shroud their villainous faces in bushy hair than to cover with decent clothing those parts of their body which required it'. Vortigern, the British king, seeking protection from these northern invaders, 'sealed the doom of his country by inviting in among them (like wolves into the sheep-fold), the fierce and impious Saxons, a race hateful both to God and men, to repel the invasions of the northern nations. Nothing was ever so pernicious to our country, nothing was ever so unlucky. What palpable darkness must have enveloped their minds - darkness desperate and cruel!'.

The passage is full of ironies. Five hundred years later the Norman invasion gave rise to the powerful historical myth of England 'before the Norman yoke', a land of free independent smallholders. How perspectives change! Reading Gildas reminds us that Britain is a country of migrants – for the Celts themselves, of course, supplanted an earlier people. They are not the original 'Britons'. The Angles and Saxons whom he deprecates were part of a huge movement of peoples, possibly prompted by climate change, which undid the Roman ecumene, and did much to shape Europe as we now know it.

Many waves of invasion or immigration have characterized human history: the Muslim expansion from 630 onwards; the Mongol invasions of the thirteenth century; European colonization after the late fifteenth century. In addition countless millions have moved more peacefully, likewise seeking economic improvement, refuge, or driven by famine and natural disaster. I want to propose a Toynbee like thesis that in the rather brief period of recorded history there are periods of great movements of peoples and more settled periods, periods of consolidation. It is true, of course, that no culture is 'pure' and that all contain elements from others. A global perspective on cultures is, in Jonathan Friedman's words, of a kind of leaky mosaic in which cultures run over their edges and flow into one another, and therefore what I have called consolidation could never be stasis.[1] At the same time, without long periods of rootedness, regional languages and cultures could never have taken shape. Languages and cultures are not made in a day: like buildings we shape them and then they shape us. People develop a profound love for their place, their language, their culture: we come to have la belle France, Ma Vlast, Mother Russia or India. It is especially important to note that the self expression of culture in language is not co-extensive with nationality. We have only 160 or so nations but more than 3500 languages and language is, I would argue, the heart of culture.

Some thinkers, like Richard Sennett, argue that humans are by nature eccentric. Judaeo Christian culture, he comments, is at its very roots about spiritual dislocation and homelessness. 'Our faith began at odds with place, because our gods themselves were disposed to wander'.[2] The BCC Asylum principles 'recognize that our lives are a pilgrimage in which we have no abiding city' and that 'our true citizenship is in heaven.

1   J. Friedman *Cultural Identity and Global Process* London : Sage 1994 p.212.

2   R.Sennett, *The Conscience of the Eye*, Norton, New York 1990 p.6.

We therefore do not attribute absolute value to the rights and privileges of nationality and citizenship'. Karsten Harries has argued that the old sense of dwelling was part of a situation where place meant destiny, and that it is a good thing to be free of it.[3] 'To be genuinely at home in this world, we have to affirm our essential homelessness...every attempt to step into the true centre, to come home in this sense...denies the essential eccentricity of human dwelling – an eccentricity that needs to be thought in relation to a centre, but a centre that withdraws whenever we seek to seize it.'[4]

Against these emphases is the importance of what Deuteronomy calls 'rest' which Gerhard von Rad highlighted in an article written in 1933, the year the Nazis came to power in Germany. 'Rest' is about security. Thus the narrative of Joshua concludes with it:

> Thus the Lord gave to Israel all the land that he swore to their ancestors that he would give them; and having taken possession of it, they settled there. And the Lord gave them rest on every side just as he had sworn to their ancestors (Josh 21 43/4).

'Rest' and possession of the land are bound up with each other. As von Rad puts it:

> It is emphasised that redemption is a present reality and that all Israel is the chosen people; and it is evident that this notion of the land which Israel is to inhabit...is a theological concept of the highest order...*We must not spiritualise any of this: this 'rest' is not peace of mind, but the altogether tangible peace granted to a nation plagued by enemies and weary of wandering. It is altogether a direct gift from the hand of God.*[5]

This is well said, and it is especially important if we are thinking about the position of migrants. Norman Habel finds in the patriarchal narratives an 'immigrant ideology' where 'land is a host country where immigrant ancestors find God at sacred sites, discern promises of future land, and establish peaceful relations with the indigenous peoples of the

---

3   K. Harries, *The Ethical Function of Architecture*, MIT press, Cambridge Massachusetts, 1998 p. 162,168.

4   Harries, *Function* p. 200.

5   G. von Rad, *The Problem of the Hexateuch and other Essays*, Oliver & Boyd, Edinburgh 1966 p.95 My italics.

land'.[6] Abraham fosters a way of life which mediates blessing and creates peaceful relations with the owners of the land, the Canaanites. At the same time the overall vision of the Hebrew bible is settlement, rest. Some degree of rootedness, or rest, I would argue, is essential to human flourishing.

'In our Midst'

I want to write now about the 'in our midst' of the conference's title. We all know that the theme of the exile in Egypt constituted a fundamental ethical guideline for Israel in many directions, and not least in relation to the refugee: 'When an economic migrant (stranger) resides with you in your land, you shall not oppress the economic migrant. The economic migrant who resides with you shall be to you as the citizen among you; you shall love the economic migrant as yourself, for you were economic migrants in the land of Egypt' (Lev 19.34). This is from Leviticus which probably comes from the post exilic period, perhaps from the brief period between the decline of Babylonian power and the assertion of Seleucid hegemony. But from the same period is Ezra: Shecanaiah son of Jehiel, of the descendants of Elam, addressed Ezra, saying, 'We have broken faith with our God and have married foreign women from the peoples of the land, but even now there is hope for Israel in spite of this. So now let us make a covenant with our God to send away all these wives and children, according to the counsel of my lord...Take action, for it is your duty, and we are with you; be strong, and do it.' (Ezra 10. 2-4). And from a century or so earlier, 'When the LORD your God brings you into the land you are entering to possess and drives out before you many nations — the Hittites, Girgashites, Amorites, Canaanites, Perizzites, Hivites and Jebusites, seven nations larger and stronger than you - and when the LORD your God has delivered them over to you and you have defeated them, then you must destroy them totally. Make no treaty with them, and show them no mercy. Do not intermarry with them. Do not give your daughters to their sons or take their daughters for your sons, for they will turn your sons away from following me to serve other gods, and the LORD's anger will burn against you and will quickly destroy you. This is what you are to do to them: Break down their altars, smash their sacred

---

6   N. Habel, *The Land is Mine: Six Biblical Ideologies*, Fortress, Minneapolis 1995 p. 135.

stones, cut down their Asherah poles and burn their idols in the fire'. It's not exactly multiculturalism.

The worry of these writers is that Israel will lose its identity. In adopting the cultural mores of other peoples it will lose sight of YHWH. These passages might be understood in relation to the Coca Cola culture, or whatever else you call the culture of globalisation, but they are worryingly close to those Muslim critics who talk of the 'corrupt bog land of Western culture' and who want to put huge bombs near night clubs.

Leviticus, or one strand in Leviticus, takes a different line which takes a position which we are much more comfortable with but even that assumes an identity between what we would call church and people, religion and culture. This is problematic for us. We would probably want to say that the church is under an obligation to welcome the stranger but in fact the burden of welcome falls not primarily on church, but on a whole culture. We can expect church to take the lead in welcoming the stranger, as it does today in many parts of the United States, in helping illegal immigrants. But in doing so it will often be behaving counter culturally, behaviour springing from a strong sense of who it is. In saying the creed and reading its scriptures church constantly reaffirms its identity. This might not be the case with a culture for a culture's sense of itself might be significantly more in question. This is important because it is with nations and cultures as it is with individuals: if you do not know who you are you cannot give yourself. Of course, 'I am who I am in relation'. But I am thinking here of pathologies. In particular I am suggesting that the current burst of homogenization is a cultural version of Alzheimer's disease which robs us of our identity. I am suggesting that only people who know who they are can welcome the stranger. When we say 'in our midst', of whom are we speaking: church or culture?

Culture as a whole, I want to argue, is not out with the guidance of the Holy Spirit: I read the Pentecost story as the endorsement of individual cultures. The Holy Spirit does not speak Esperanto but every culture hears the gospel in its own native tongue. What this means, argued Herder, is that cultures are irreducibly distinct and that their uniqueness is a divine gift which can by no means be compromised. 'Not a man, not a country, not a people, not a natural history, not a state, are like one another. Hence the True, the Good, the

163

Beautiful in them are not similar either'[7] Each image of humanity is unique and *sui generis.*[8] Each represents an aspect of divine giftedness. Different cultures represent different forms of imagination, ways of looking at things, forms of social organization, senses of humour and psychological and moral energies but all represent a response to the one Spirit.

From a theological point of view this might underlie protest against the Westernisation of non western cultures. Nor must we think simply of cultures grouped around language: even within language areas regional cultures vary very significantly as do class and occupational cultures. Gender inflects every culture.[9] There are a great many cultures, in this sense, always shaped by others, which provide their context, and remain their points of reference so that almost all cultures are, and always have been, multi-culturally constituted.[10] These hugely varied cultures represent in different ways aspects of human flourishing. We have learned from Common Ground to speak of this aspect of our being as 'local distinctiveness' and, as I say, we can understand it, though not undialectically, as part of the Spirit's gifting.

Today this local distinctiveness is threatened throughout the world: 'If on arriving at Trude I had not read the city's name written in big letters,' wrote Italo Calvino in *Invisible Cities*,

> I would have thought I was landing at the same airport from which I had taken off. This was the first time I had come to Trude, but I already knew the hotel where I happened to be lodged...Why come to Trude I asked myself. And I already wanted to leave. 'You can resume your flight whenever you like' they said to me, but you will arrive at another Trude,

---

7   Herder, Einzelne Blätter zum 'Journal der Reise', *Werke* IV p. 472.

8   Herder, 'Ideas for a Philosophy of History', *Werke* XIV p. 210,217,230.

9   John McGrath speaks of his upbringing in Wales and Liverpool, and his courtship in the Highlands and his awareness of the multiplicity of British culture. 'Each one of these cultures...has to me a totally distinct landscape, an emotional and linguistic and interpersonal specificity, a distinctness from every one of the others which is complete, yet with a variety of contiguities' John McGrath, *The Bone Won't Break: On Theatre and Hope in Hard Times* London: Methuen 1990 p.54. We can replicate this the world over.

10 Bhikhu Parekh, Rethinking Multiculturalism: Cultural Diversity and Political Theory Basingstoke: Palgrave 2000 p. 163.

absolutely the same, detail by detail. The world is covered by a sole Trude, which does not begin and does not end. Only the name of the airport changes.[11]

The sense of homogenisation is part and parcel of the whole process of globalisation, of 'space-time compression'. The old sense of place which belonged to the period of consolidation was maintained by the sheer difficulty of travel and communication. The new conditions tend to undo the sense of place. The airport Calvino describes is part of a galaxy of 'non-places' – motorway service stations, shopping malls – remote from the dense marking of a historic community. Place is replaced by non place. What it means to be local changes. A few control and initiate 'flows' and 'movements' but the vast majority have no say in what happens. In a globalized world, says Zygmunt Bauman, localities lose their meaning-generating and meaning-negotiating capacity and are increasingly dependent on sense giving and interpreting actions which they do not control.[12] The locality no longer belongs to the people who live there but to those who 'invest' in it, people who are not bound by space, and thus constitute a new class of absentee landlords.[13] In this case what does 'in your midst' mean? I take it that Ezra and Deuteronomy have some such worries in mind.

Against such developments Sue Clifford and Angela King want to celebrate local identity. In their book *England in Particular*, published last Christmas, they write: 'Places remain vital through absorption and reinvention. In Northamptonshire compare a deep-ploughed field of a hundred acres with ten fields of ten acres. Read the richness in the latter – perhaps medieval ridge and furrow overlaid with Enclosure hedgerows, never ploughed or strewn with herbicide or fertiliser. Go to the East End of London and compare a sixties, seventies or eighties estate with the Huguenot buildings, bagel shops, and Bangladeshi restaurants of Brick lane and the mosque in an old synagogue that was once a chapel. Local distinctiveness must be about history continuing through the present, not about the past.' Note that local distinctiveness is not about a fossilized view of the past. The book is arranged

---

11 I. Calvino, *Invisible Cities* London: Vintage 1997 p.128.

12 Z. Bauman, *Globalization: The Human Consequences* Cambridge: Polity 1998 p.3.

13 Bauman, *Globalization*, p.10.

alphabetically and 'mosques' and 'diwali' are a part of England in particular. They go on: 'The crude sacrifices made by comprehensive and rapid change demean us. We can add without brutalism. Dynamism and vitality should be great allies of local distinctiveness. Attempts to arrest both progress and decay in a Cotswold village or in culturally diverse Leicester risk the danger of creating a frozen moment, the real place and people having sunk below waves of preciousness or poverty. We must hold on to the old while demanding the best of the new'.[14] If, as William Blake argued, God is to be found in minute particulars, then resistance to homogenisation follows from the Church's understanding of a world shaped by God. In this respect the command to hew down altars and smash sacred poles might have something going for it, though again, it sounds suspiciously like destroying the World Trade Centre.

Is it possible to affirm local identity without being chauvinist? The claim that it is rests in the dialectic of universal and particular, which has many different construals, including, today, the discourse of human rights. The Christian account of universalism and particularism, is rooted in the incarnation. The understanding of incarnation hammered out in the fourth to the sixth centuries was not the product of scholastic perversity, but a struggle to know how to be true to the gospel in a milieu foreign to its origin, the milieu of Hellenism. The formulae of Nicaea, Chalcedon, or of Leontius of Byzantium do not, as critics allege, offer us a dated, culture specific and alienating account of what it means for God to become human so much as a set of guidelines for thinking about the engagement of the Wholly Other with human particulars. They are, as it were, the grammar of divine cultural engagement. In the fifth century debates, for example, the Antiochenes fight for particularity and the Alexandrines for universality. As has always been recognised, the formulae which constituted the truce between them do not give an account of *how* the universal and the particular can be combined, but simply set out the rules of engagement. Any failure to respect the claims of either universal or particular, it was claimed, is unworkable.

---

14 Sue Clifford and Angela King *England in particular* London: Hodder and Stoughton 2006 p xi.

The doctrine of the incarnation, I wish to claim, offers us a way of affirming both universal and particular in a non-alienating way, in a way that does not involve false particularism. Universalism and particularism are equally true, and without either one we lose our humanity. This commits us, on the one hand, to a resolute defence of local distinctiveness at every level: languages, cuisines, building styles, customs and so on and so forth. Where these are life giving they represent a response to the Spirit of life. A theology of culture is at the same time a theology of the Spirit, about God active in the historical process, not a God asleep or unconcerned. If God exists then God acts, and that action must call forth results. The life-affirming aspects of culture, I am arguing, are those results. At the same time that very conviction commits us to a universalism, to the cherishing of what Herder called *Humanität* everywhere. No policy informed by incarnation can be universalising if this means the elimination of difference. Equally, no cultural policy informed by incarnation could be chauvinist.

As Peter's experience in the house of Cornelius shows, Pentecost was an endorsement of a pluralism in which no culture is unclean, all can provide access to God, and no culture is the exclusive norm of truth. The One gospel becomes meaningfully mediated through the 'Many' refractions of culture and historical contingency.[15]

Mission

No culture represents a full or perfect response to the Spirit of God. The gospel is, in a fundamental way, about metanoia and any encounter between the gospel and culture involves a call to change, to die to all that is not worthy of humanity in their traditions, but then to rise in greater splendour. This call to change is permanent. We cannot envisage some cultures which are 'Christian' and others which are not. Once again it is with cultures as it is with individuals and churches: all need to confess and to change the whole time. In this context 'mission' is the address of the Word of God to all people, calling to repentance and new life.

---

15 Lamin Sanneh, *Encountering the West: Christianity and the Global Cultural Process: the African Dimension* London: Marshall Pickering 1993 p.149.

'Mission' originated in the resurrection and Pentecost: it was about spreading the good news of the death of death, of the overcoming of alienation, of the possibility of a new type of human community not marked by class, race and gender divides. To use Paul's shorthand, it was about the overcoming of 'sin'. The new community, 'church', was at the heart of this mission. Not that the new community was itself the sum of the gospel – that was about God and God's act. But without the new community the gospel could be neither preached nor seen in action. The difficulties this involved led Augustine to talk of a distinction between the invisible and the visible church. The church is both the source of mission and always at the same time needs to be missionized itself. From the beginning it has involved itself in compromises and contradictions which made its mission impossible. The creation of 'boards of mission', for example, led to the loss of the perception that the church itself was missionary, and was part of a movement of cultural retreat in which the church became introverted and, in the post-colonial era, preoccupied with apology. But the church has always known it lives by forgiveness; this fact is part of the secret of its carefree joy. Authentic mission is the sharing of this joy.

How does all this apply to 'strangers in our midst'? Let me make two suggestions based on the work of two teachers, one African and one Asian, who have thought profoundly about these issues. Lamin Sanneh distinguishes two basic ways of mission, which he calls diffusion and translation. The first is to make the missionary culture the inseparable carrier of the message, so that the new religion is implanted in other societies primarily as a matter of cultural identity. In his view Islam works in this way. The second is to make the recipient culture the true and final locus of the proclamation, so that the religion arrives without the presumption of cultural rejection. This is mission by translation.[16] Translation, he notes, entails a distinction between the essence of the message, and its cultural presuppositions, with the assumption that such a separation enables us to affirm the primacy of the message over its cultural underpinnings. What Sanneh calls 'the essence of the message' here is the core proclamation of the gospel. But what might this be? Many Christians identify the core of the gospel as sin and redemption through the sacrifice which Christ's

---

16 L. Sanneh, Lamin *Translating the Message: The Missionary Impact on Culture* Maryknoll: Orbis 1989 p. 29.

death constituted. I would rather say that the cross stands as a marker of human resistance to the divine will there displayed, and as the unique sign of the direction of the divine love. Paul characteristically moves from the event of crucifixion (Gal 3.13) to the claim that 'in Christ' the categories of race, class and gender no longer count (Gal 3.28). The 'in Christ' is shorthand for the movement which stems from Christ, the task of which is to live out and witness to the breaking down of all barriers. It is a vision of human history, bound together first 'in Adam' – subject to the law of violence, and then 'in Christ' – subject to the law of peace, or reconciliation, a vision of a *process*. Mission is about trying to persuade people of the deep rootedness, the cogency, of this process as it springs from the events surrounding Jesus. From the very start this suasion has involved healing and hospitality, welcoming the stranger.

My second teacher, Aloysius Pieris, finds the core of the gospel in the claim that in Jesus the irreconcilable antinomy between God and Mammon and the irrevocable covenant between God and the poor is made flesh. True evangelism is to live this out in fellowship with the authentic spirituality and liberative dimensions of other religions (and, we can add, other cultures, including secular ones). What we need to be liberated from are the things that cannot give us freedom. The church has to experience solidarity with non Christians by witnessing to the spirituality common to all religions (by practising the beatitudes); and reveal its Christian uniqueness in proclaiming Jesus as the new covenant by joining the poor against Mammon's principalities and powers that create poverty and oppression.

Pieris warns that the liberating spirituality of the religions is gradually being extinguished by the wave of capitalistic techniculture that has begun to shake the religious foundation of all cultures. 'The market economy (which thrives on the quest for profit) and consumerism (which plays to our accumulative instinct) have enthroned Mammon where, once, the human person and the human community as well as the earth on which we live, were the sole beneficiary'. Lesslie Newbigin agrees with him. The eighteenth century, he remarks, found in covetousness not only a law of nature but the engine of progress by which the purpose of nature and nature's

God was to be carried out.[17] This represented an inversion of the entire Christian witness up to then. 'Growth' became the watchword. But growth for the sake of growth is a form of cancer. 'In the long perspective of history, it would be difficult to deny that the exuberant capitalism of the past two hundred and fifty years will be diagnosed in the future as a desperately dangerous case of cancer in the body of human society.'[18]

To put these two visions in other terms we might say that mission is about sharing the vision of a world and therefore of human life based on free grace, on service rather than power, on peace rather than violence. This bears on our theme of strangers in our midst in a particular construal of what is today called multiculturalism. This is the view that different cultures correct and complement, educate and civilize each other. Strangers are therefore welcomed into our midst acknowledging what they bring to the enrichment of our own understanding and ways of life. Bhiku Parekh advocates a multiculturalism driven by a spirit of critical self-understanding which would open up a theoretical and moral space for a dialogue with other ways of life in a common search for a deeper understanding of the human project.[19] To this self evidently humane proposal we have to put two questions. The first is that, as Lesslie Newbigin pointed out, people of one race may include diverse cultures and religions, and people of one religion can embrace a vast variety of races and cultures. The idea of multiculturalism is therefore much more complex than is often supposed.[20] Secondly, it is also clear that multiculturalism easily functions as a screen for global capital. It adopts the empty global position of the corporation and, just as the post-modern dismissal of metnarratives conceals the metanarrative of the market, so multiculturalist respect for the other's specificity is in fact a way of asserting one's superiority.[21] The way to fight ethnic hatred effectively, he argues, is not through the negotiation of difference but

17 Lesslie Newbigin, *Foolishness to the Greeks*, London: SPCK 1986 p.109.

18 Newbigin, *Foolishness* p.114.

19 Parekh, *Multiculturalism* p.111.

20 L.Newbigin, L. Sanneh, J. Taylor, *Faith and Power: Christianity and Islam in 'Secular' Britain* London: SCM 1998 p.5.

21 Slavov Žižek, The Ticklish Subject: The Absent Centre of Political Ontology London: Verso 1999 p.216.

proper political hatred, hatred directed at the common enemy, by which he means capitalism.[22] Rather similarly it is argued that the multicultural agenda papers over the problem of racism. Like those forms of Christianity which make reconciliation prior to justice, it cultivates the illusion that dominant and subordinate can somehow swap places and learn how the other half lives, whilst leaving the structures of power intact.[23] Under the terms of the multiculturalist consensus, write Gita Sahgal and Nira Yuval-Davis, fighting against racism is reduced to preserving the 'traditions and cultures' of different ethnic minorities. 'Cultural differences between various groups in society become of paramount importance, rather than tackling the central problem of racism itself: unequal power relations which bring about 'modes of exclusion' inferiorisation, subordination and exploitation.'[24]

This highlighting of the question of power in multicultural issues is important. Bound up with this is a commitment to pursue the truth. Christians, Newbigin argued, must welcome plurality but reject the ideology of pluralism. They have to argue for the public truth of their beliefs, but in a way that is prepared to meet, and be convinced by, the truth of others' positions. For Newbigin what is unique about the Christian gospel is that those who are called to be its witnesses are committed to the public affirmation that it is true and are at the same time forbidden to use coercion to enforce it – an ironic point given Christianity's history.[25] For him it is only the gospel which enables us to affirm both that God has made God's will and purpose known and to affirm that God has ordained a space in which disbelief can have the freedom to flourish.[26] In the Christian life it is liturgy which is our school of attention, for discerning seeds of the Word is a practice which has to be learned. In this school we can learn how to narrate a story which neither totalises nor relativises but, in Gerald Loughlin's words, 'imagines the possibility of harmonious difference and peace as

---

22 S. Žižek, *The Fragile Absolute* London: Verso 2000 p.11.

23 Cited by Barnor Hesse, *Un/settled Multiculturalisms* London: Zed 2000 p.8.

24 G. Sahgal and N. Yuval-Davis Introduction in *Refusing Holy Orders* London: Virago 1992 p.15.

25 Newbigin, *Faith and Power* p.148.

26 Newbigin, *Faith and Power* p.159.

the inner dynamic of the Triune God'.[27]   In imitation of that conversation which is revealed within the Trinity, Christian life is intrinsically dialogical.[28] Engagement with people of other faiths (and cultures) is informed by a vision of the Trinitarian God who acts as both host and guest, as the great Rublyev icon suggests. In our present world situation, characterised by mass migration and by the mingling of populations living by radically different mores, that, I suggest, is probably what we mean by mission.

27 Michael Barnes, *Theology and the Dialogue of Religions* Cambridge: Cambridge University Press 2002 p.28.

28 Barnes, *Dialogue*, p.228.

Chapter Eleven

Multicultural Worship: Theological reflections on experience

Thomas R. Whelan

This chapter is modest in its intent. It simply seeks to bring together personal experience and that of others in relation to multi-cultural worship, and examine this in the context of ecclesiology and theology of worship. The theme of this book, 'mission and migration', gives rise to many considerations, especially as these impinge on a practice central to us all: our weekly worshipful gathering to offer praise and thanksgiving to God in Christ Jesus. While this reflection has in mind primarily migrants who are Christian, it will point to areas in which hidden and unintended discriminatory practices among the dominant membership of our churches might be less than supportive of the fundamental human needs of all migrants, such as security, identity, belonging, and a sense of being in control of their own destiny. Reflection will be grounded in the experience of the various churches on these islands and will attempt to contribute some critical comment on the ecclesial and liturgical implications of what it means to welcome 'the stranger in our midst'.

The issue here is not simply one of hospitality or even 'mission' (understood narrowly as evangelisation) but rather of who are we and what are we as 'church' and how we articulate communion/*koinonia* within a local church which is characterised by cultural and sometimes linguistic pluralism. An unexpected pre-requisite, as we will see, involves a move from a sense that the congregation or assembly is a cosy place where we will remain undisturbed, to an openness to the need for repentance and reconciliation, particularly within the receiving church community, along with a preparedness to undergo conversion.

There is nothing innocent or romantic about the concept of multicultural worship, which requires the negotiation and re-negotiation of many issues. While sociology and other human sciences will assist, it is the faith context which supplies the raison-d'être of the gathering of the congregation that will actually point a way forward to us. Like the term 'democracy', multiculturalism has many expressions, not all of which are equally commendable, and all of which are somewhat problematic but yet preferable to a number of the alternatives available. The sociological need for a hegemony – the presence of a dominant group – brings out what the American liturgical theologian, Mark Francis, calls the '"dark side", the perennial human quest for dominance and control over people who are "other", which besets people of all cultural backgrounds'[1]

Ecclesiology and Eschatology

There is a Christian world-view which should inform how we approach the many issues relating to multi-cultural worship. Our mission as Church is to be instruments of the *missio Dei* which is described in 1 Timothy 2:4 as leading all people to the great truth of the graciousness of God who desires nothing else for us other than wholesomeness and the fulfilment of the deepest desires of our created being – all of which is to be found in our entanglement in the primordial and ultimate relationship of the Trinity.[2]

The high moment of the completion of the *missio Dei* is described in that most liturgical of books in the bible, the Book of Revelation, in terms of a wonderful Banquet of the Lamb where the great multitude of humankind is gathered to sing the praises of God:

> After this I looked, and there was a great multitude that no one could count, from every nation, from all tribes and peoples and

---

1   Mark R. Francis, "Multicultural Worship: Beyond Cultural Apartheid and Liturgical Esperanto," in *The Renewal That Awaits*, Eleanor Bernstein and Martin F. Connell, eds. (Chicago: Liturgy Training Publications, 1997), 39.

2   See my "'The Liturgy is Missionary': Elements of a Fundamental Liturgical Theology of Mission," *Faithful Witness: Glimpses of the Kingdom*, ed. Joe Egan and Brendan McConvery (Dublin: Milltown Institute, 2005), 357-375, which describes elements of the theological relationship between liturgy / worship and mission. On pp 359-360 and note 7, I describe how 'salvation' is understood through various layers of the meaning of the Greek word *soteria* and the Latin term *salus*.

languages, standing before the throne and before the Lamb (Revelation 7:9: NRSV).

The eschatological destiny of humanity could not be more clearly depicted.[3] If we pitch alongside this an opening sentence of the 1964 document on the Church from the Second Vatican Council, we can see something of a world-view which demands an investment from us in our dominical gatherings:

> Since the Church in Christ is a kind of sacrament, that is, a sign and instrument of the intimate union with God and of the unity of all of humankind ...[4]

The language here is bold. In traditional terms, a sacrament not only points towards the deeper reality it signifies but is also instrumental in bringing about that reality which it purports to represent. The Church is to be an instrument or an agent for achieving the union with God and the unity of all humankind. The Church is also the environment within which the rehearsal of this unity and union takes place, and, if it is faithful to its role, the locus of a foretaste of things to come. The local congregation or assembly will give expression to this to the extent that it will allow, in Kingdom fashion, those on the margins of society to be the chief guests at the Sunday eucharistic banquet; to the extent that it will welcome and embrace the stranger; and to the extent that it will move beyond its own comfortable space and permit the multiculturalism in worship described by Revelations chapter 7.[5] The opening sentence of *Lumen gentium* might offer a wonderful theological insight, but is costly when

---

3   The new Jerusalem with a new heaven and a new earth is described in Revelation 21:1-4 (see also 2 Corinthians 5:17).

4   Second Vatican Council, Dogmatic Constitution on the Church, *Lumen gentium*, 1 (my translation).

5   The biblical foundation for this is succinctly given in the *Policy Statement on Racial Justice*, 2003, no 7, of the Churches Together in Britain and Ireland, published in *Redeeming the Time: All God's People Must Challenge Racism* (London: CTBI Publications, 2003), 4-5: 'God has a special love and concern for the poorest and most vulnerable and for those who are seeking asylum and safety (Psalm 146:7-9). At the onset of his ministry, Jesus cited Isaiah (chapter 61) in his proclamation that his essential role was to bring justice for the oppressed (Luke 4:18-19). Paul declared that the kingdom of God is not to do with cultural customs but with justice (Romans 14:17). Essential features of justice are full inclusion and participation in the life of the community, as distinct from being marginal and not fully belonging. (For example, Deut 10:19; Lev 19:34; Romans 12:13; Hebrews 13:1-2).'

it comes to its realisation. There is a very real link between church on earth and *ek-klesia* of those who have gone ahead of us.

The multicultural assembly is first of all gathered as God's people, chosen, royal and holy so that it might proclaim 'the mighty acts of God' who called it 'out of darkness into God's wonderful light'. Once a non-people, it is now God's people (see 1 Peter 2:10-11). This biblical vision calls for incarnation within the church assembly, painful as it might be:

> We believe that the church must be committed to challenge racism and discrimination in all its forms. We recognise the common guilt (however unintentional) in colluding with the evil of racism by our own actions and by not examining and questioning structures and patterns within our church family life.[6]

The ecclesial significance of the worship-gathering is precisely in the fact that we assemble so as to be inserted into the saving paschal mystery of Christ through Word and Banquet, through which we repent and receive forgiveness so that the reconciliation of all creation in God (eloquently described by Paul) be accomplished and shown forth as a foretaste in our Sunday congregations. Ecclesiology and eschatology must embrace in liturgy.

Forms of Multicultural Interaction

The American theologian John Coleman studied how political establishments in history and today dealt with cultural differences in their midst, and offers a taxonomy of strategies for their management.[7] He sees eight different strategies within political and other groupings. Four of his eight ways 'for dealing with ethnic group differences in a society of culturally pluralistic subgroups' attempt to manage differences, while the others represent ways of eliminating cultural differences.

---

6 Baptist Union of Great Britain, *We Belong Together: Policy Guidelines on Racism*, 1994, quoted from *Redeeming the Time*, 16.

7 John Coleman, "Pastoral Strategies for Multicultural Parishes," *Origins* 31 (2001): 497-505.

The first two strategies of elimination are radical: genocide and forced massive population transfers – both of which we still encounter in the world today. The third is 'partition or secession into separate states' (the Czechs and Slovaks after the fall of communism; the North of Ireland in the 1920s).[8] The fourth strategy to eliminate differences is assimilation. The problems that assimilation as a policy brings are well known and manifold. Again Coleman:

> Note well, assimilation proposes the eventual eradication of cultural differences! Assimilation has, until quite recently, been the preferred strategy in democracies, such as Britain, France, Australia and the United States. Immigrants might be allowed in, for economic or humanitarian reasons, but it was assumed that in relatively short order they would learn the language, adopt the rules, customs and mores of the host country. Acceptance of outsiders was predicated on their "becoming like one of us". Hybridity, the hyphenated character of a Pakistani-British or a Korean-American was, at best, tolerated as a brief way station until the foreigners became, *tout court*, French, Australian or American.[9]

Coleman then goes on to list four strategies for managing differences rather than eradicating them. The first of these is what he terms 'hegemonic control' best exemplified, he claims, in the Ottoman and Austro-Hungarian empires, both of which were authoritarian and hierarchical societies. This method would permit, for instance, the use of other languages, religions or even indirect rule, maybe even honouring subordinate forms of ethnic and religious leadership in legislation, but 'the ultimate rule was by the ruling group'. He makes the observation that 'there is a partial sociological necessity for some common culture' and that, irrespective of a desire to have all cultures treated with equanimity, cultural theory and sociology tell us that there will be a dominant or hegemonic culture.[10]

Another method is that of territorial, quasi autonomy in a federalist system, not unlike what obtains with Quebec in Canada. There is also

---

8   Coleman comments that 'in principle, partition/secession can be a viable and just solution to national cultural differences': "Pastoral Strategies for Multicultural Parishes," 498.

9   Coleman, "Pastoral Strategies for Multicultural Parishes," 498.

10 Coleman, "Pastoral Strategies for Multicultural Parishes," 499.

nonterritorial autonomy (*consocialism*) similar to what is now found in the North of Ireland, with 'reserved seats in Parliament or partial veto powers or government subsidies in support of schools and communal institutions for subordinate groups'. Finally we have 'multicultural integration' which Coleman calls a 'rare phenomenon' and describes as '*structured* acceptance of cultural difference within a political community'.[11]

Coleman appeals to the reflections of the Canadian philosopher Charles Taylor to help unravel some of the issues which emerge in how the term 'multicultural integration' is interpreted.[12]

(a) The dominant liberal model of jurisprudence currently found on the North American continent cannot respect difference or allow for group rights. Such a philosophy of law states that equality can only come about when there is a uniform application of how rights of people are defined, and it is suspicious of collective goals. The interests of ethnic groups are in 'recognition, identity, language and cultural membership'; whereas this dominant liberal political philosophy only respects the individual before the law. And this law must be the same for everybody. The logic of this philosophical view-point continues to affirm the legitimacy of people's cultural identities, but it makes these private concerns which have no place in the public forum. However, it needs to be noted that we are not dealing here with a supposedly 'neutral' set of principals, but rather a philosophical and cultural understanding that reflects one dominant, hegemonic group. What, in effect, we have here is discrimination, even if this is wholly unintended.

(b) An opposite view-point to that represented by the liberal political model is one in which we must 'recognise and even foster peculiarities (because all people, in fact, do inhabit particular groups, identities, and they treasure them as what makes them who they are)'. Otherwise they, in effect, are told that they have nothing to offer to society, that they are part of a society which is culturally homogenous – something that they know to be untrue.

---

11 Coleman, "Pastoral Strategies for Multicultural Parishes," 499.

12 I offer here a synopsis of the summary that Coleman gives of Charles Taylor's position as expressed in some of his more recent writings: see, "Pastoral Strategies for Multicultural Parishes," 499-501.

(c) Taylor observes that modern democracies, to survive, need common identity, a sense of mutual trust, and common sentiments and identity. This sociological need means that while democracies 'herald their inclusiveness (government by, for and of all the people), in fact, democracy has historically also been exclusive of cultural minorities'. This has meant that, in practice, most democratic states have, in fact, worked with a policy of assimilation. Again, Taylor:

> Most migrants want to assimilate substantively to the societies they have entered, and they certainly want to be accepted as full members. But they frequently want, now, to do this at their own pace and in their own way, and in the process they reserve the right to alter the society even as they assimilate, they want to codetermine the future of the societies they have entered.[13]

(d) Taylor proposes that it is possible to have a form of multicultural integration that does not require full assimilation. The requirement for this is based on the understanding that 'humanity is realised not in each individual human being but rather in communion among all humans, in and through their viable cultures'.

A number of things happen in the process of multicultural integration:

- the first is an acknowledgement that when migrants enter a new culture, they seek assimilation, but in a way that does not deny their own identity. There is a tension between wanting to belong and realising that they are different. The cultures they bring with them do, in fact, change from the ones they leave behind.

- allowing groups to form their own cultural organisations allows newly arrived peoples a sense of security in their new environment. If this does not happen they are left with a sense of total powerlessness. With their cultural grouping, they feel that they can integrate into their newly adopted culture without having to accede always to the terms of the majority culture. It also helps people preserve something of their ethnic identity as best they can.

---

13 Charles Taylor, "Democracy, Inclusive and Exclusive", *Festschrift* for Robert Bellah, quoted in Coleman, "Pastoral Strategies for Multicultural Parishes," 500.

- Coleman observes:

> A society with no hegemonies is probably a utopia. A simply multicultural society is an anarchy, unliveable. But multicultural integration leaves space and agency so that, in the eventual fallout, the immigrants will retain some genuine sense of their identity and gain respect for it, and also deal with the host culture (if not in total equality, which would be a mirage), at least as agents who have voice and will change what they enter as they, in turn, are changed.[14]

Multi-cultural Worship and Its Many Expressions

All churches on these islands have, in various ways, become involved in forms of ministry to migrants, from the setting up of Welcome Centres and other services to the invitations to join us in our weekly worship. However, a more sustained reflection on what we are doing is warranted, lest we misdirect our energies or unintentionally recreate the very problems of identity and displacement that we aspire to resolve.[15]

The Presbyterian Church in Ireland articulated well this dilemma:

> However, despite policies of integration and programmes of community relations, experience has underlined the gap between vision and reality. Diversity easily disintegrates into fear, suspicion, hostility and violence. [...] for the Christian the diagnosis is sin, in both persons and societies. "[Churches] are obliged to confess that racism is a sin, not only of individual Christians, but of churches and societies at large. People have become accustomed to patterns of neglect of and contempt for others, of injustice and prejudice, of degradation and exploitation, and now regard them as 'normal'."[16]

---

14 Coleman, "Pastoral Strategies for Multicultural Parishes," 501.

15 Sometimes unknown to a community, racist practices can be reflected in its liturgical ritual. See my, "Racism and Worship in Ireland," in *The Stranger in Our Midst. Refugees in Ireland: Causes, Experiences, Responses*, ed. Thomas R. Whelan, Foreword by President Mary McAleese (Dublin: Kimmage Mission Institute, 2001), 53-69.

16 *Policy on Asylum Seekers and Refugees*, no 5: A Report by the Race Relations Committee to the 2003 General Assembly of the Presbyterian Church in Ireland (Belfast: Church House, 2003), 3-4; citing *Racism in Theology: Theology Against Racism*, Report of a Faith and Order Consultation (Geneva, 1974), 7.

Before we outline forms of multicultural worship, an important observation regarding the way migrants align themselves to churches needs to be stated. The Irish Methodist minister, Alan Martin, made the important observation that throughout Europe the established or predominant church in each country has often been unable to receive members with a different cultural and confessional background.[17] He states, for instance, that in 2002, there was an estimated 20 multi-cultural congregations and Christian fellowships in Ireland, that is, those with at least 25% of membership from the newly arrived migrants, and that these are generally not to be found in the majority churches on the island.

This fact alone challenges the larger churches into reflection on what it does in relation to migrants, and how it does what it does. Some of the challenges can be identified easily, others less easily. Coleman emphasises the fact that multiculturalism is not always comfortable, and that culture is almost always a place of conflict. To acknowledge conflict leaves open the possibility of growth and a forward movement, one that will benefit all involved. To downplay conflict or cover it over will be to withdraw from the process of multiculturalism and to move towards – however unintentionally – covert assimilation. A second reflection is that there is need to find ways to speak to one another and to the theology of the majority. Church, like democracy, needs some common shared language and sentiments to tie together its separate communions. There has to be a

---

17 Martin gives some examples: in Norway the Lutheran church is the established church with 86% membership of the population, "yet only a relatively small number of migrants have joined. The Catholic Church, on the other hand, has become a multi-cultural church [there]. In Germany there are only a small number of multi-cultural congregations. In Holland [The Netherlands] the Moluccan Christians, who came from former colonies from 1951 onwards, 'received very little attention from the established churches on their arrival' [see J.M. van Kruis, "The 'multi-cultural' society and the churches in the Netherlands," *Culture Divides - the Gospel Unites?* (Brussels: The Churches' Commission for Migrants in Europe, 2002), 71]. These were mostly Reformed Churches. In England the first wave of immigrants in the 1950s who came from the Caribbean were not welcomed to the extent they should have been by the established church. There are now a number of multi-cultural congregations mostly in the South of England. In Ireland the pattern has been similar. It is the smaller churches in the Republic of Ireland that have been more successful in welcoming members from different backgrounds." In, Rev'd Alan Vincent Martin, *"The Ephesian Moment.* The Possibilities of Cultural Reconciliation in a Cosmopolitan Environment".* Unpublished M Phil Thesis submitted to the Irish School of Ecumenicist, Trinity College, Dublin, in 2003, pp. 26-27.

common shared culture too if a multicultural church will not become a sheer anarchy.[18]

All churches admit or aspire towards forms of multicultural worship and integration, yet various forms of this pose their own problems. Among the more common expressions are the following:
- sharing space with other churches
- sharing space with same church denomination
- ethnic churches / parishes
- liturgies in common
- multicultural liturgies

Common to all of these expressions is the desire to create space for fellow Christians in the migrant population so that they will be able to give expression to their faith in Christ Jesus.

We will consider only some of the general issues which emerge from the experience of multicultural worship. But before we do so we should reflect briefly on effective cultural interaction.

The type of welcome we offer must be Christian at its deepest level. The extension of a welcome to migrant Christians is not simply that of visitors to our house but of our brothers and sisters in Christ, and thus of our equals. Christians from different ethnic backgrounds must eventually come to a sense of ownership, which includes participation in an empowering leadership team and ministry which would co-ordinate matters in the parish.

Effective cultural interaction requires that three goals be striven for, according to Robert Schreiter. The first is simply to recognise the other and the difference that this brings. Because it makes us feel uncomfortable, we often prefer to ignore it. Secondly, this difference needs to be respected for what it is rather than simply acknowledged. To merely note it can be patronising, and this could mean that difference is temporarily tolerated in the hope that it will eventually disappear. Respect, however, means that difference is valued in its own right and that it adds to the richness of the world. Schreiter notes that it often takes a long time to come to this level of respect, since people are prone to see difference as deviation from (their) norm or as

---

18 See Coleman, "Pastoral Strategies for Multicultural Parishes," 501.

a failure to reach their level. The final goal to achieve is a 'healthy interaction among cultures'. This implies a willingness to be changed by the other and to incorporate aspects of that otherness into one's own cultural world. It allows the perspectives of another culture to change one's world view. Ultimately, these three goals will help to lead migrant members of churches to feel that they are more than simply guests, that they do, in fact, 'belong'. And 'belonging is a fundamental human need since we are by nature social beings'.[19]

Emerging Issues at the Margins of Multicultural Liturgies

The liturgist Mark Francis identifies two extremes to be avoided in the expression of multicultural worship. The first emphasises the uniqueness of each ethnic group and encourages it to develop its own form of worship. The second discourages the separatism that is essential to the term multiculturalism, and promotes a single pattern of worship which permits expressions of the various cultures represented but on the understanding that the fundamental unity of the congregation is respected. What is needed is a balance between these two emphases.

Well-meaning practitioners of what Francis calls 'cultural apartheid' ensure that minority Christian groups worship apart in order to create space so that they retain their cultural identity and be thus saved from assimilation.[20] Ethnic parishes/churches would be an example of this type of cultural apartheid. These are acceptable only to the extent that they underline the identity and security of the minority groups in an otherwise culturally hostile environment. But, it must be noted, these also serve to keep the groups apart thereby slowing down the process of integration.

There seems to be a need to retain a balance between separation of groups and their integration, and this is a difficult task to achieve. When separation is presented as the goal to be achieved, or to be the best way among a number of bad pathways, then the process of integration will not happen, or else a form of assimilation into wider society will take place which will be fraught with difficulties. These

---

19 See Robert Schreiber, "Ministry for a Multicultural Church," *Origins* 29 (1999): 1-8.

20 See Francis, "Multicultural Worship," 41.

difficulties would stem from there being no opportunity for people to gain a sense of their cultural identity in the safer environment wherein such differences are respected and given value (through separation) rather than in the wider society where, desirous of conformity, assimilation is aspired to and difference tolerated by the migrant.

But the journey to this position is delicate and needs to be reflected upon. Rowan Williams articulates a concern for respect which is at the heart of this debate:

> The liberal assumption that 'treating everyone alike' is the answer rests on a view of human nature which is deeply problematic. It assumes that there is a basis 'inner' humanity, beyond flesh and skin pigmentation and history and conflict, which is the same for all people. But human existence is precisely life that is lived in speech and relation, and so in history: what we share as humans is not a human 'essence' outside history, but a common involvement in the limits and relativities of history. The only humanity we have is one that is bound up in difference, in the encounter of physical and linguistic strangers. [...] When great stress is laid upon our oneness 'under the skin', there is always the risk of rendering that as 'this stranger is really the same as *me*' – which subtly reinforces the dominant group's assumptions of the right to define. The norm is where I or we stand. This risk is one reason for looking very hard at the goal of 'treating everyone alike'. It represents the worthy and correct commitment to avoid discrimination that overtly disadvantages or distances the stranger; but it can fail to see the prior need to allow them *be* strangers.
>
> But the liberal's anxieties have some point. Careless talk about proper distances, allowing the independence of another's story and perspective, and so on can be costly, for at least two reasons. The 'licensing' of difference, even the practices of positive discrimination, on the part of the dominant group will fail to move things forward if it is simply a concession that does not alter the basic realities of power in the 'public spaces' shared by the dominant and subordinate groups. Or, in plain English, the dominant group's own possibilities have to be affected by this process if there is to be real change. [... The

second point is that] it is actually impossible in any imaginable future world that human groupings should be able to pursue their goals in total mutual independence: 'separate development', by whatever name, is a fantasy. ...[21]

Back to worship. As a medium-term goal, separate forms of worship do not reflect the reality of people gathered for worship. Through migration they have embraced a new reality, a new cultural context within which to live their own cultural identity, a different way of living, and an impingement of cultural and maybe even religious values different to those of the 'home' culture. Their lives, as Francis says, 'are characterised by a multicultural reality that needs to be reflected in the liturgy'.[22] To try to replicate the worship patterns of the home country is an exercise in cultural archaeology and nostalgia – maybe required at an initial stage of coming to a new culture, but not helpful in the medium or long term. Part of the purpose of gathering for worship is to allow us place our story (a present reality) into redeeming contact with the 'God Story' where reconciliation, enablement, grace and forgiveness become part of the dominical movement of praise and thanksgiving that is so central to the rituals of worship and without which a gathering for worship loses meaning.

The other extreme is characterised by what Francis terms 'liturgical esperanto'. At times the creation of a multicultural liturgy is akin to the exercise that Ludwik Zemenhof undertook in the creation of the artificial language, Esperanto. The parcelling out of various elements reflective of different ethnic groups, rather than having the intended effect of making everybody feel included and part of the assembly, can have the opposite effect of alienation. According to Francis, the reasons for this are simple and many. Firstly there is the question of who decides, and on what criteria are decisions made as to what cultural elements are included? If the dominant group make these choices, then there can be a legitimate accusation of tokenism. Choices are often made on the grounds of what seems to be *different* to the dominant group, and this can be patronising. There is also danger that changes made are done from the ritual template of the dominant

---

21 Rowan Williams, "Nobody knows who I am till judgement morning", *On Christian Theology* (Oxford: Blackwell, 2000), 282-3.

22 Francis, "Multicultural Worship," 43.

group, which means that the influence of minority cultural groups is at surface level and is superficial to the experience – and this is the way (again, unintended) that the group is now made to feel about itself. Secondly, such a liturgy – because artificially constructed from diverse cultural elements – is divorced from life.

According to Francis, 'it is important, then, that all involved in multicultural ministry be clear that their primary ministry is to help a diverse community celebrate the paschal mystery of Christ experienced here and now in a multicultural setting, not to celebrate cultural diversity as the objects of our worship.'[23] In this time-consuming process which demands patience and pastoral leadership, the fragility of the migrant group needs to be addressed in a wholesome way so as to help it find its own voice and space.

Conclusion

Multiculturalism in its many forms is challenging and demands that real issues in the cultural process be addressed by all groups. When this falls prey to a superficial form, cultural difference is denigrated and it is reduced to exotic items such as food and dances.

The Presbyterian Church in Ireland outlines the challenges and contributions of multicultural worship:

> Many asylum-seekers and refugees are Christians. A survey just completed for the Irish Council of Churches documents the significant contribution being made to church life, sometimes within mainline denominations, more often through both newly founded ethnic churches or new church fellowships. It also describes some of the genuine difficulties of Christian communities with very different cultural backgrounds relating to each other.[24]

---

23 Francis, "Multicultural Worship," 47. For Francis, the rootedness of the ministry and liturgical expression is essential: 'Liturgy is never an exercise in abstraction if it is truly understood as the work of the people. A *sine qua non* for multicultural liturgy preparation is inquiring about the material conditions of the people and the tensions and positive interactions that exist among people in the parish. Liturgy prepared without a sense of where people are often becomes as artificial as Esperanto.' Ibid. 45.

24 *Policy on Asylum Seekers and Refugees*, no 15: A Report by the Race Relations Committee to the 2003 General Assembly of the Presbyterian Church in Ireland (Belfast: Church House, 2003), 13.

However, worship only takes place in the context of a wider life, and this is outlined in an uncompromising way in this same Policy document. It is only in the context of the wider ministry that churches give to migrants in a multicultural society that the question of multicultural worship can be adequately dealt with: 'Individual Christians and congregations can foster understanding and counter uninformed prejudice in their local community'. The Presbyterian policy statement lists at length the many broad issues that churches need to attend to, and conclude by advocating that wider society should be educated in the various matters that relate to migration: 'We urge our local congregations to seek out or set up adult education programmes covering such matters'.[25]

The Christian aspiration is that all will be able to experience in life the embodiment of the Pauline insight,

> For in the one Spirit we were all baptised into one body – Jews or Greeks, slaves or free – and we were all made to drink of one Spirit (1 Corinthians 12:13: NRSV).

---

25 *Policy on Asylum Seekers and Refugees*, no 16; pp. 13-14.

MISSION

and

THE NEXT CHRISTENDOM

Edited by Timothy Yates

Responses to Philip Jenkins, **The Next Christendom: the Coming of Global Christianity**, Oxford 2002

Papers by Werner Ustorg, Vinoth Ramachandra, Viigo Mortensen, Stephen Spencer, Darrell Jackson, Valentin Dedji, Kathy Ross, Allen Yeh, Stephen Skuce

Cliff College Publishing, 2005
ISBN 1 898362 38 6
£12.99

Other BIAMS Conference books:

Mission: An Invitation to God's Future,

ed Timothy Yates

Cliff College Publishing, 2000

Essays by Jurgen Moltmann, Theo Sundermier,
Anton Wessels, Timothy Yates, David Smith,
Kirsteen Kim, Philip Thomas

ISBN 1 898362 25 4

Mission and Spirituality:
Creative Ways of Being Church,

ed Howard Mellor and Timothy Yates

Cliff College Publishing, 2002

Essays by David Hay, Saunders Davies, Robert Kaggwa,
Brian Stanley, Peter Ward, Laurent Magesa, Michael Crowley,
Esther de Waal, John Burgess, Craig Gardiner

ISBN 1 898362 28 9

Mission – Violence and Reconciliation,

ed Howard Mellor and Timothy Yates

Cliff College Publishing, 2004

Essays by Robert Schreiter, Cecelia Clegg, David Porter,
Drew Gibson, Kenneth Ross, Margaret Raven, Jacques Matthey,
Kenneth Fleming, Andrew Wingate

ISBN 1 898362 32 7